HOLES IN TIME

by Frank Costantino

ACCLAIMED BOOKS
Box 18186
Dallas, Texas 75218

Distributed to jail and prison inmates throughout North America by International Prison Ministry, Box 63, Dallas, Texas 75221, (214) 494-2302.

All characters and situations in this book are factual but some names of persons and locations have been changed to avoid damaging careers or reputations of others involved, many of whom are now living exemplary lives.

Holes In Time

ISBN #: 0-932294-06-5
Library of Congress Catalog Card #: 79-89370

Second Edition: 1986

Printed in the United States.

DEDICATION

To Chaplain Max Jones who has the courage to put God first, and the salvation of lost souls as his primary goal. In the day of negative thinking about the role of the prison chaplain, Max Jones stands as a shining example of Christian faith at work behind prison walls.

. . . and to all the staff and directors of Christian Prison Ministries and prison workers everywhere.

. . . and to Dr. Richard Leoffler, Dr. Donald Brown, Curt Bock and Dan Horton who believed in me from the *very* beginning.

. . . and to my wife of 17 years, Cheryl, who went through the whole prison experience with me.

TABLE OF CONTENTS

BOOK 1

Part I

Part II

Part III

BOOK 2

FOREWORD

Frank was a professional criminal. He deliberately decided to be a thief and a robber. With protection from the underworld he preyed on the upperworld. In eleven years he participated in robberies and thefts totalling eleven million dollars.

All this he did with no qualms of conscience. He reasoned that bankers and businessmen stole with their pens. He stole with his guns. He saw no difference.

On his first felony conviction he received a sentence of 22 years in prison. There he had plenty of time to think and to reason within himself. The inhumanity that he witnessed demanded that he find out what he wanted to be, a giver or a taker. He reached the conclusion that those who don't care leave holes in time.

His personal encounter with Christ in the office of Chaplain Max Jones settled all the issues. He had found the answer to life's most important questions.

This book is distinctly unique in taking you with Frank through the inner thought processes that led to a gangster becoming a dedicated Christian.

Chaplain Ray
Director, International Prison Ministry
Dallas, Texas

GLOSSARY

Breaking bad:	playing tough
Chaser:	guard
Copping deuces:	pleading his case
Hack:	guard
Iron pile:	weight-lifting equipment
Offed:	killed
Piece:	knife, weapon
Stand-up guy:	reliable person
Stash:	hiding place
Sword:	knife
Touch-hog:	tough guy

INTRODUCTION

"A very daring expose of prison life and one man's battle with himself to find real meaning to life. I believe anyone will find this book thought provoking and brutally true, while at the same time warm and excitingly human. 'Jesus is the answer, the only answer,'" says Max Jones, Chaplain in the Florida Penal system.

Chaplain Jones, who was elected as Chaplain of the Year at the American Correctional Association of Congress of Corrections, 1976, has served in the Florida penal system for the last 16 years. Through his ministry, some of the most hardened prisoners in this system have given their lives to Christ.

The list includes Austin Brown, a former alcoholic who currently is serving as Chaplain at Florida State Prison, Jack (Murph the Surf) Murphy, and international jewel thief, Bob Earler, super cop from Hollywood, Florida, who was convicted as the "Catch Me Please Killer," and the author, Frank Costantino, "a heavy weight criminal who stole millions."

BOOK 1

As told to John Caldwell

Part I

"Be not deceived; God is not mocked:
for whatsoever a man soweth,
that shall he also reap.
For he that soweth to his flesh
shall of the flesh reap corruption . . ."

Galatians 6:7-8

1

This was going to be my last big robbery. It would put me on easy street for the rest of my life.

I'd been uneasy about it ever since we started out this evening. Not that good kind of concern that keeps a guy on his toes during a job but a deeper uneasiness than I'd ever known before. I racked it up to my promise to my wife, Bunny, to quit this business and so we moved in.

Walking quickly along behind the expensive shops which lined Coral Gables' Miracle Mile, we passed right by Adrian Thal's Fur Salon, our ultimate goal. In a specially constructed vault inside that store hung some $5 million in furs. By tomorrow, they would be on a freighter headed for a market far away from Miami.

In checking out the alarm system installed in Thal's, we discovered there was no way of making direct entry into that building from the roof or alley. We couldn't do it through Roal's next door at 348 Miracle Mile either but Allan Abess Ltd., at number 340, was an easy entry. So that's where we went in.

We had a truck parked right across the street from the police station, which was only half a block away. In the alley behind the stores, it might have raised questions, especially on Easter morning. It was now eight o'clock on Saturday night and we planned to be loading by noon Easter day. We had the walls between the three stores to go through and then we had to go through the roof of the vault which was free standing within the building.

We wore black leather gloves, were armed, and carried star drills, chisels, saws, hammers and rubber mallets to soften the sound of the blows as we cut through the block walls between buildings.

It was a cool job. No fuss, no place for slip-ups, carefully planned. We had blue-prints of all three stores.

We knew the ADT set ups. We knew where everybody who worked in all three stores was and where they would be until Monday morning. We knew the patrol schedules. We knew each other. We already had a buyer for the furs. The truck was waiting, the ship they would go out on was waiting. It was a cool job. That was my signature.

It was a far cry from my first job. That netted me $500. I was fresh out of the Navy with a Bad Conduct Discharge, dirt poor, almost unemployable, with no skills and hungry for the "good life" I saw other guys living.

I could see what went on in the world. I was walking around the edge of the Boston underworld. I saw that the guys who had it had it because they took it. I used to stand on the street corner and watch them go by in the back seats of their black Cadillac sedans, expressionless, exuding power and class, as if one of the hoods up front was a uniformed chauffeur.

And I would kick the litter in the gutter with my beat up shoe with the hole in the sole and dream of scoring big. I wanted to be a gangster.

Now some people wanted to be a doctor and some

people wanted to be a lawyer but not me. I wanted to be a gangster and I wanted a Cadillac, not a T-Bird, I wanted a 4-door, black Cadillac and I wanted to be a gangster.

I finally stepped out and made my first move. A robbery. Five hundred dollars.

Boy! Did that feel good! My first score, I liked the feeling of taking what I needed, doing something about where I was. I was doing what I had to do and I had $500. It was alive in my pocket.

I felt good. The job had taken nerve—I had it. I went downtown and bought some leather Italian shoes and a silk suit and a white tie and went back down to the same corner I was hanging around on the day before. There's something about nice threads, makes you feel together.

The police got wind of the new money I had, the flash of the new threads and the heat came down. I got busted and sat around wondering who had ratted me out. I was still green but had it together, they wouldn't get me to cop out. They'd never stick that rap on me.

And I beat it. Scott free. And the guys I hung with, they thought I was cool too. I was a stand up guy, I went to the station and told nothing, no one else got busted. I decided that the only problem I had was that I hadn't established a prosperous image with the police. Once that was done, I thought, they wouldn't hassle me. I'd be okay. Things were together.

So I set my sights higher. That $500 had really made me feel good and it just stood to reason with me that if $500 had really made me feel that happy, $1,000 would make me twice as happy. Now, I'm not a college graduate but that just made sense to me.

Twice as happy.

So I stole a thousand dollars. And I was absolutely right. It made me twice as happy. I was together, things were under control.

We took turns cutting through the walls. The two guys who were with me, Lennie Feldman and Ralph Goodman were strong guys and we made good time. We found we couldn't go through the ceiling of the vault, so by ten Easter morning, we were cutting through the door of the vault. Hidden in the door of that vault was a single, unmapped alarm connected directly to the police station.

I was on the main floor at the back of the shop and looked out and there were police everywhere. I grabbed the phone in the office and called Bunny to tell her I was about to be arrested and she should call my attorney. When I got her and told her where I was she said o.k. and hung up on me. She was hot. They had 13 policemen and two dogs out there by the time they told us to come out.

The trial was a farce. I mean, there we were, caught in the building, stuff we'd left in there scattered through three stores. They had us cold and with our street reputations there wasn't a chance for plea bargaining. After all, they had set my bond on one B & E, with no previous felony conviction, at $45,000.

We went to bat. It was a farce. We knew we'd be found guilty but the only way we could keep me out of prison was to go the appeal route. Plead innocent now, then try to build into the trial reversable errors, for appeals. We were also counting on the cops lying for the D.A.'s overzealousness or a witness not showing up, to help us along.

Well, I was found guilty. I got 15 years for

breaking and entering with intent to commit a felony. I received two and a half years for attempted grand larceny and then I received five years for possession of burglary tools. Then the clincher came. The time was to be served consecutively. Twenty-two and a half years for my first felony offense.

I was burning inside, seething with anger. My attorney, Ron Lynch, had guessed the most I would get would be a five to ten year stretch, which meant that if, after all of the appeals, I ever did end up going to prison, I'd be out in three or four years if I stayed cool.

Cool. That was the word. Cool.

I asked Ron, very quietly, "What happened to the five-to-ten?"

"No worry, Frank," he said, typical of lawyers. "Don't worry! That sentence and the consecutive bit just gives us a stronger bid in the appeals. The sentence itself is not legal."

"I don't have to tell you," I said to him, "that I don't want to serve any of that time. What happens now?"

"We're going to appeal when he asks us if we want to," he answered, "and here's the motion for setting the bail." He held up a couple of typewritten pages. "You'll be out on bond again in 24 hours, maybe less."

"What'll my bond be?"

"Oh," he said, "with him in this mood, high. Maybe as much as $20,000." That was a lot of dough in the mid-sixties. Then he added, "If he sets it any higher than that, that'll really show the prejudice of the court and I'll include that in the appeal."

I thought, "Unh, hunh. That appeal junk again."

I'd never been involved in an appeal before. In the back of my mind I was beginning to wonder if this guy was stroking me.

The judge took the motion for bail and set it down on the calendar for the next day. That night in the Dade County Jail, I wasn't so sure. I was moved over there about four or five in the afternoon. It was about eleven at night now and I was lying there on my bunk. I remember being surprised at discovering what I was thinking, what my mind was doing as if it was another mind, as if I had two minds, one of them me and the other a sort of independent mind that could comment on me or think about me in some sort of separate way, yet at the same time.

What I was surprised at was that this other mind was thinking, "Well, I've got seven hours in on a twenty-two and a half year sentence. Now, I wonder how many more hours I've got left to do?"

Inside me, I wasn't cool. I felt as if I was tied down to that bunk and I had a cold prickly feeling up the back of my neck and little sweat beads at the roots of the hair at the top of my forehead.

The jailer who had let me into the holding cell had said to me, "They really got you this time, didn't they Frank. This one will stick."

He wasn't nasty about it, wasn't digging at me. It wasn't like he was kicking a dog that was down. It was just a matter of fact, like he was saying my license tag had expired or something.

Ever cool, I came back, "Stick where, old man? You know where you can stick this 22½ years, don't you?"

And now the very hours of that 22½ years were laid out before me. What was . . . let me figure. 24 hours in a day, 365 days in a year, twenty-two and a half years. I tried to multiply all of that out in my head and the prickly sensation got worse ... and that whole immeasurable amount of time stretched out in front of me like a road stretching on and on and on, out to the horizon and then up into the air and on and on and on into infinity, a narrow road, bounded on each side by prison bars and it had a slick ceiling and there was a bright light running down the middle of the whole ceiling and it burned all of the time, just like the light in the hall outside my cell, which would burn brightly through the bars all night long.

It was hot in that cell, close, and there was an odor, the odor of jail. I came to know it as prison odor. Bunny used to just take any clothes I had been wearing when I was picked up and held a day or two, which was often because they were always harassing me, and just throw them away because of the odor, she just couldn't get that odor out of them.

It was an odor made up out of frustration and fear, bodies close together, with no sun, 20 men shut up in a cell, psychopaths, murderers, perverts, all in one stinking hole made for 13 men. Eight slept on the floor.

Weak guys made an odor all their own, an odor of urine and tears and self-pity and their own fear. Sometimes there was an odor of blood and semen.

The next day, the judge set the bail at $50,000. I posted it and hit the street again. It was now November. I had been arrested in Adrian Thal's back in April and had been on the street ever since except for the last two days. I'd kept busy while I was waiting for the trial. I'd stolen several million dollars worth of stuff during that time.

There were three murder raps they were trying to

pin on me, murders that took place while I was free awaiting trial. I had also had a lot of harassment. I owned a respectable business. We manufactured plaster-of-paris items for home decoration. The cops just never left me alone, though. Every time I turned around, I was being picked up for some screwy charge they were trying to tack onto me.

My lawyers now began to go the appeal route. I still kept busy on the street. Then one night, while I was going to pick up my brother, I got stopped. I wasn't even in my own car, I was in Bunny's car. And I got stopped and they searched her car, without permission, and while they were searching it, they planted a pistol under the car seat and I'm framed on a charge of a convicted felon carrying a weapon and I'm back in the Dade County Jail again.

About this time some glory happy reporter at the *Miami Herald* writes a long story about bonds. It begins on page one and continues on the inside to six columns and the headline on it reads: Is Appeal Bond A Work Permit? Then this joker proceeds to tell about seven "professional hoods" who have been arrested for another offense while out on bond for some conviction.

Talking about me, the article said: "Frank Costantino, a former prep star (I was captain of my high school football team), has been had for many things dating back to April, 1962.

"The crimes, with which he has been charged locally, range from breaking and entering to possession of burglary tools and, the most recent, assault with the intent to commit murder.

"Police records show that Costantino was convicted in Massachusetts for larceny and served one year in 1963 in the Billerica House of Correction.

"Although convicted in the 1966 Adrian Thal burglary in Coral Gables and sentenced to 22½ years in Raiford, he has managed to remain free on appeal bonds.

"At the time, Costantino, a former Hialeah High football player, and two accomplices (one of them the notorious Lennie Feldman) were caught in the Adrian Thal store, he was out on bond on two Hialeah counts of receiving and concealing stolen property.

"The Hialeah charges were later thrown out of court by Criminal Court Judge Carling Stedman on the motion of Costantino's lawyer to 'suppress evidence.'

"At the time of his arrest in the Coral Gables burglary, Costantino was charged with three counts of breaking and entering with intent to commit grand larceny at three Miracle Mile stores.

"While free under bond, pending appeal of the long prison sentence he drew in the case, police reported that Costantino 'has kept busy' and found time to open up a business in Hialeah."

The least important thing that happened as a result of this was that the Hialeah-Miami Springs Chamber of Commerce voted unanimously to rescind my membership.

Another part of the article read: "Is there no protection for society from the professional hoodlum convicted and sentenced to prison? Can the appeal bond be denied?"

"State Attorney Richard E. Gerstein thinks the professional should be considered in a different light than the non-professional.

"In view of the record which indicates persons are committing crimes while out on appeal, it seems to me the courts should take a tough hard look at this situation," he said.

"This would increase the number of those required to remain in jail while their appeals are pending—particularly the hardened criminals."

And it went on with more of the same.

The end result was that the judge said, when they brought me in on the trumped-up gun charge, "I've had it with this guy. I'm just going to pull his bond." They pulled my appeal bond, I was sent back to the Dade County Jail and my attorney went to Tallahassee to the Supreme Court to get the order changed.

He got an order from a Justice of the Supreme Court saying I was to be released on my bond again. The Miami judge, Carling Stedman, refused to change his orders and Capt. Jack O. Sandstrom, chief of the sheriff's jail division, was caught between the conflicting orders on what to do with me.

While everybody was arguing back and forth about what to do with me, Judge Stedman told the sheriff he wanted me on the next available transportation to Raiford, where the major state prison was located.

At 4 a.m. the next morning, a guard came to my cell in the Dade County Jail to get me and took me into a room with a bunch of other guys and then they were feeding us grits and gravy and I realized they were sending me to Raiford.

"Hey, wait a minute," I said to one of the deputies, "You guys can't send me anywhere, I've got a Supreme Court order calling for my release. You guys are making a mistake."

"We don't make mistakes," some wise guy cracked, "You are the boys with the mistakes."

They were now lining us up, ready to march us down the hall. "Wait a minute," I said, "I want to talk to my lawyer. You can't send me out of here like this without me talking to my lawyer."

"No phone calls," this sergeant said. "You're under court commitment to be transported, so no phone calls."

"So okay," I said. I walked to the bus and got on.

They call it the Gray Goose. There were about 40 other guys on the bus with me. It was a portable jail. We had a toilet in there and that was all. Even the driver was fenced off from us.

There was still one seat left by a window when I got on and I took it. Anger seethed through me as I sat down.

It had never entered my mind that the court, that those stupid deputies, would ignore a Supreme Court order. I *knew* I was being held against the order of that court and I couldn't believe it was possible for them to do this to me or to anybody. I really knew, now, what it felt like to be shanghied. The law is not their rule any more than it was mine. There was an unnaturalness about the way I felt that was unnerving and as I began to settle down into the rhythm of the swaying bus and realize that I was actually going to prison, other fears and apprehensions began to edge into my mind.

It was a cold February day, February 1968. Dawn began to lift the darkness from the roadside as we rolled along and I looked at the other guys on the bus. I knew a few of them, small-time hoods from around the county. None of my crowd.

Soon we were passing through small towns and little knots of men and women at street corners would stare at us as we passed, disgust spread over their righteous faces.

I flinched from their condemning stares, then wondered why I felt that way. All they were seeing was some skin and hair stretched over some meat and bones. They weren't seeing me because they didn't know me. Why should I care if they looked at what they could see? They'd never see me again. It wasn't as if they could tie what they saw to Frank Costantino.

They didn't even know my name. All they knew when they looked into that bus was that here was a bunch of guys going to prison. They didn't know who was who. Suckers, they probably believed that everybody in the bus was guilty, that everybody was going where they deserved to go, that "the country" would be better off without us.

I wondered how they would feel if they knew their beloved "system" was corrupt clear to the core. I wanted to yell at them, "The Supreme Court says I'm supposed to be free!" So much for the Supreme Court. Well, I knew before now that you could only get the justice you could afford to buy. Apparently, I hadn't been able to buy enough. So much for all of that constitutional crap. The "system" does what the system wants to do.

I'd known all of that before. I knew that the way you got treated depended on the clout you had. I had the clout, I just hadn't had a chance to use it the way they yanked me out of jail without me even being able to see my lawyer. If they wanted you in Raiford, you went to Raiford.

Well, guys had gotten out of Raiford before. I had

been in a lot of places which were designed to keep people out, no reason I shouldn't be able to reverse that and get out of a place designed to keep people in.

I looked back at the face staring into the bus windows and I thought to myself, I'd much rather be in jail as a "has-been" than on these streets of these hick towns as a "never-was."

I suddenly began to think about my business, about Decor Originals.

Who was going to answer the mail today?

When would Bunny find out about me and go down there?

Who was going to fire that stupid Roger before he wrecked the casting machine completely?

Who was going to decide whether to use that new plaster or not?

Who was going to get the money out of the safety deposit box to meet Friday's payroll?

The frustration of being beyond the place where I could reach out and do anything enveloped me.

Some of the old-timers on the bus were telling their seat-partners what to expect when we got to Raiford. I could hear them, all around the bus, telling wild tales to some of the younger prisoners.

"They'll take us to the West Unit. That's where everybody goes when you first go in. They give you talks about what's going on and they are kind of like classes," one of them was saying.

"They're a bunch of red-necks," another joined in.

"Yeah, and when we first get there, they are going to search us, so be clean. You ain't never been searched until you've been searched coming into the West Unit," another said. "They've got it down to a science."

"You be careful," came another voice from the back of the bus. He was talking to a young boy. He had given him so much guff that he had all of the young guys around him so revved up they were ready to bust the first guy who was so much as just plain friendly to them.

"Yeah and you can get raped easy up there too," another said.

The guy sitting next to me said, "That guy's a real joke. He should know about rape, that's where his head is. Some of today's daddies are yesterday's queens."

They kept yakking away and I began to get drowsy. I snoozed briefly and when I awoke, I sensed a new feeling, a quietness, an anticipation in the bus.

Looking through the front window I saw the cause. What looked like miles of hurricane fence, topped with barbed wire stretched away on our left in both directions. Behind it were more fences and inside them the solid buildings and smokestacks of what could only be Florida State Prison at Raiford, and, beyond it, Union Correctional Institution.

Soon we could see the guards in the towers and then, barely slowing down, we rolled right through the gates and by the time the bus stopped, we were deep inside the prison, at the West Unit.

A guard unlocked the bus door.

"All right, you guys, stay right where you are," he said.

He didn't really have any trouble with guys who were jumping up and down to get out to go through those doors behind him. Even the guys who were coming "home," the repeaters, the two-time losers, or three-time or four-time or whatever, who had more pals in here than they had out on the streets, sat where they were.

"Okay, boys," he said. He did something funny with the way he said the word "boys." He gave it two syllables and made it sound like it was a dirty word. "Ya'll get off the bus and line up over here. Line up and answer up as I call your name."

"Okay boys. Adams, Clinton."

A tall, thin young man, seated ahead of me on the bus answered.

"Allen, Henry," the guard called. I already hated the very sound of his voice.

Allen answered, "Yes, sir."

"Back again, huhh?" The guard looked him up and down, frowning. "You ain't never gonna be no good to nobody, are ya' Allen?"

Allen didn't answer but waited quietly till his name was checked off the list.

"Braxton, Joseph."

A huge black dude yelled, "Yes, sir" and had his name checked off.

"Costantino, Frank," the guard called.

"Here."

"Yes, sir." The guard shouted it so loud his voice cracked and the "sir" was a shrill, falsetto sound.

I'd been in jails enough to know their game, so I said, "Yes, sir." These jerks would never get a sir straight out of me. They just breed hate with their crap.

A sudden wave of apprehension came over me. It was a mixture of fear of the unknown and the frustration of being checked in like an object. The building before me was my new home and it didn't feel right at all, but even here, I was cool. I followed the line as the door jerked open and walked through. I was in prison. The door shut behind me.

2

We were in the classification center. I knew it was going to be a trip. Not as bad as some of the old-timers on the bus had said, not as good as some of the virgins thought it might be.

"All-right, boys," a guard yelled, "Line up in front of this door."

"Okay, boys," he said, swinging the door open into the next room.

"You all go in there and move over to them tables by the wall. Then strip, put your free world clothes in them paper bags on the table and your shoes over on that counter.

"Then you all move through this door into the shower room," he drawled, "and then we'll tell you what to do next as you come out of the showers." He spoke so slowly we could have done half of what he said while he was saying it.

I stripped, folded my clothes, put them in the bag, returned them to the counter and went to the showers. After the shower, we got dusted with DDT for crab lice.

"Raise your left arm, boy," the guard on my left said. I raised my left arm and the nozzle of a duster moved under my armpit as the guard drove the plunger in and a cloud of DDT hit and engulfed me.

"Keep walking," the other guard barked. He was a

little guy, but he was ordering us around that room like he was a giant.

"Unh hunh," I thought. "Put a uniform on a momma's boy and he'll walk up to you like he's ten feet tall."

"Raise your right arm over your head," he said.

I did and another blast of DDT surrounded me.

"Turn your back to me," the guard said.

I turned my back to him.

Again the fog of DDT. As I straightened up another cloud caught me in the back of the head.

"Turn around and face me," the first guard said. "Shut your eyes, hold your breath till I tell you to breathe."

I could feel the clouds of dust hit me as I heard the plunger drive down the barrel of the duster.

"Okay, boy, breathe," he said after a few moments.

I took a deep gulp of air, choked and opened my eyes to find my head still in a boiling swirl of DDT.

A low, mocking laugh erupted from the guard.

Anger surged through me as I responded to another order to move on. "Look at these clowns," I thought, "working for minimum wage in a place like like this just so they can wear a uniform and feel big!"

"Okay, boys, get dressed," one of the guards called.

I moved to the table and began to put my clothes on. As I did, Frank Costantino began to die. I looked around me. Everybody looked just alike. The shoes looked like farmer's shoes. Me, Frank Costantino, in farmer's shoes! I looked like the kid that used to come to my plant to wash windows. Even the blue shirt and the pants were the same.

Only where his said, "Florida Window Cleaning," mine now read "20952."

In Miami, I was used to wearing Hickey-Freeman suits and Stacy-Adams shoes . . . alligator shoes . . . and here I was, a guy that looked like a window cleaner.

I really felt for the first time that I had 22½ years to serve and that it would probably be at least ten or eleven years before I could get out of there. I felt like I was either dead or dying, headed into another sphere of time.

It was as if I had stepped into another world where everything existed, yet nothing existed. A world where reality was something static, an object out there beyond those fences somewhere and that all of this that was happening to me was real too, but in some different and unbelievable sense . . . in another dimension maybe.

After we were dressed we checked our free-world clothing into the property room and told them where we wanted it sent. We got to keep some stuff of our own, but not much . . . only what was on a list they had on the wall. You could keep a watch but I couldn't keep mine because it was too expensive. I'd have to wait until Bunny sent me a Timex or something.

It took me days to quit looking at my left wrist everytime I thought about the time.

Next, we were sent through the yard to a dorm where I was given a bunk. It was, I thought at first, just like the Navy. But it wasn't like the Navy. In the Navy you were a person. You weren't just a number.

There was a lot of Mickey Mouse stuff in the Navy, true, but that's just what it was, Mickey Mouse stuff, comic stuff. It wasn't so much that the guards were intentionally cruel to you . . . it was something worse . . . they didn't care.

Some of them talked right through you, like you weren't human and didn't have any feelings.

As I went through the hours and days of classification and orientation where we were told what we could not do and what we could do . . . there was almost nothing we *could* do . . . it became more and more obvious that there was no way I could stay in this place and build the kind of time that I was looking at.

No way . . .

I began to look at ways of escape. At the options. Every possibility I considered ended at a dead end. I did it just as if it was a job outside I was getting ready to do. Checking every angle, leaving no room for errors, making sure all of my calculations were right, detail after detail after detail.

Plan after plan had to be abandoned because each one of them required including other people in on the escape and I couldn't depend on anyone else. Getting outside the walls had been done many times, but a successful escape means getting away completely after you'd gone over.

At night we'd lie in our bunks and talk about getting out and how much time this one had done and how much time that one had done or what another guy was going to do when he got out.

This was going on one night and this old guy down the row said, "What's the difference? They all come back."

"What do you mean," I asked, "they all come back?"

"They do," another guy who was serving his fourth stretch answered. "If they don't get caught within the first few days, which is mostly the way it is, they'll be back in a little bit, with another sentence for more time for the escape."

He looked around him at the guys in the dorm, and added, "Most of these guys, even you first timers, are serving a life sentence now . . . only they are going to be doing it two or three years at a time."

Well, I wasn't serving any life sentence on the installment plan. They'd never catch me again, that I knew. Just let me once get out.

It didn't take me long to learn about the different classification levels in the various institutions and what each meant in terms of the kind of custody which was involved. From maximum custody, which was the East Unit, to closed custody, which was primarily within The Rock, to medium custody, which allows you to go to any of the prisons around the state, and there were ten or eleven of them then, to minimum custody, which allowed you to go to any facility, road prison or whatever.

They had another rating which was called statewide trusty, which meant you could go anywhere.

As I was learning all of this, I came to realize that if someone were classified to a prison where there were no guards in the towers, minimum custody, it would be a lot easier to escape than it would be from a maximum security institution like where I was.

Then one of the clerks told me that all transfers to other prisons came out of Tallahassee, so I now understand I could be in Raiford for a while even if I got a low custody classification. Well, that's what I was going to go after. So I set aside my plans to try for an escape there and began searching for ways to be transferred to an institution where I would have a better chance of getting away with it. Then I lucked out.

One morning, I had an interview scheduled with a classification clerk, Henry Cotton. As he began talking to me, it dawned on me that this guy had a lot to do with what prison I'd be put in, or could have.

So I began asking him about my options, feeling him out as I did. He began to share some things with me, telling me what went on at this prison and what went on at that prison. And he also told me what custody classification you needed to go to this prison or that prison.

As he began talking about the custody classifications, I had that second-sense feeling you get sometimes that he was telling me something else too.

So I asked him, "What do you do to get a classification, say as a medium custody guy?"

"Well," he said, "you don't get it by asking for it." He paused a minute, and when I didn't say anything, he went on, "It all depends on your record, the amount of time you're building, lots of things."

"And what does a guy like me, with my background, look like for a medium rating?"

"I'd say, off hand, not good. Course, you never know," he said. "Old Oliver, the classification officer who'll handle your case, has been known to bend the rules a bit here and there sometimes."

Now this guy knew I had some money and I knew he knew I had some money. He also knew I knew he knew I had some money. He was sitting right there looking at a form which stated how many hundred dollars I had surrendered and had been put in my account in the prison. He also knew some of the crimes I had committed, so he knew I probably had more where that had come from.

He wanted to do business with me and he was leaving open doors for that and I wanted to do business with him but I needed to check him out. Maybe this had all been too easy. So I said I'd talk to him later and I went back to the dorm.

Once there, I sent word over to The Rock to some guys over there I'd known from Miami to find out what kind of guy this Henry Cotton was. The word soon came back: he was a drug user but he wasn't a rat.

So satisfied that he wasn't a stool pigeon, I set out to meet him again.

When we were seated at his little table, I opened it up saying I'd sure like to get a minimum custody rating.

"No way," he said. "If you get a minimum custody rating within three years with your record you'll be lucky."

"Yeah?" I asked. "Well, I'd like to get closer to home, not in a close custody joint like The Rock."

"Well," he came back, "that's where you're headed, it looks like, unless something happens."

"I'd sure like to see something happen, then," I said.

"Minimum custody don't mean a transfer south, just improves the chances."

"I'll take the chance. I'd like to get closer to home, you know, for visiting."

"There's the 'O' Unit across the river too. They might send you there. Of course like I said it's easier to transfer from one minimum custody joint to another than go from The Rock."

"And what's it like?" I asked.

"It's a pretty good place. It's all two-man cells and there's a narrow room at the back of them where the roof is open so the sun can shine in. They don't count you in until ten at night, and you'd work out, probably, on a job outside the fence. I see you were a cook in the Navy, maybe they'd put you in the kitchen."

"I might like that," I said, showing just enough interest to keep the conversation going. Outside the fence job . . .

"Course with your record . . ." and he let the phrase hang there, like a smoke circle someone had blown hanging between us.

"How much help would I need to get a medium classification so I could get in there?"

"Well," Cotton replied, "We might find you some help. How much is it worth to you?"

"I dunno." Still very cool. "What should it be worth to me?"

"Well, maybe I can make a patch for you with Oliver, the classification officer I work for, but it would have to be a decent amount. Can you get me $1,500?"

"I can get $1,500," I said.

"How soon?"

"As soon as it's needed."

"Write a note."

"Wrong, get a phone call for me."

I made the call and made arrangements for Oliver to make direct contact.

"Okay man. By the time we clean up your folder, you'll look like an angel and they'll be wondering why you got sent up here in the first place." Cotton took the number, asked me a few more routine questions and that was that. I went back to the dorm to wait.

Two days later, I was called out early in the morning, fed, and two deputies from Dade County picked me up to take me back down to the Dade County Jail.

It turned out I was going back to appear in court on an aggravated assault with intent to commit murder charge. This had to do with a guy named James Arthur Gregg and an arson job at Coco John's Restaurant, a Hialeah night spot. Gregg had been charged by police with arson in the case. The guy who owned the place was a good friend of mine, but he had leased the place, license and all, to a guy I had a really serious beef with.

That resulted in a gun fight at the apartment complex I lived at. Me and Bobbie, my brother, shooting it out with these dudes who referred to themselves as the Coco John's gang. There were about 12 of them, and the shoot-out wound up in a draw with every car in the parking lot shot full of holes and Bunny inside the apartment wondering who was dead.

I vowed to get each one of those punks and James Authur Gregg was supposed to be one of them. A guy we knew, Bob Keene, tipped my brother and me off that Gregg was staying in the Everglades Motel on S.E. 9th Street in Hialeah. Keene was a stand up guy. He knew the beef and wanted in. He was close to me anyhow. A good friend. Gregg was as good as dead.

On the way over there, we saw Gregg walking along the sidewalk, a couple of blocks away from the motel.

Bobby said, "Pull over, I can get him into the car."

"Okay," I said, and pulled up to the curb. Since Gregg knew me and would be afraid of me, I turned my face away, back out toward the street as we pulled up.

As we stopped, my brother yelled at him, "Hey, Jimmy, come here. Come on, get in the car. Hurry up man, it's important."

Gregg started coming toward the car. Now it hadn't been our plan to get him in the car. Our plan had been to go into the motel and hit him in the motel, but when we saw him walking on the street we had to change our plan.

So here I am looking across the street the other way and the other two guys are yelling to Gregg to hurry up and get in the car and he's moving toward the car. Then all of a sudden, I still don't know why, he stopped cold, frozen, then bucked and ran.

My brother grabbed his gun and took off after him one way, I wheeled the car around, pulled off the road, and Keene and I got out of the car and started chasing back where we hoped to cut him down. It was dark and he was moving quick. Well, although I had several good shots at him, we missed him.

So, while Bob Keene goes on looking for him on foot, my brother and I take the car and do a couple of turns around in front of the motel. On the third turn around, there are cops everywhere and we get pulled over, dumped out, frisked and taken downtown.

Somebody had tipped detectives that there was loot stashed in the motel. The detectives checked it out and found a room full of loot from burglaries and while they were there, Gregg comes running in and tells them we're trying to kill him. So I end up being charged with aggravated assault with intent to commit murder. The next day they charged me with possession of firearms by a felon because I was out on bail on the Adrian Thal fur case.

Now I'm on my way back down to Miami to face those charges in court.

It was very interesting. They had had dozens of witnesses lined up to testify against me but when the trial came up, not one of them would testify. Gregg refused to testify on the grounds he might incriminate himself and the whole case fell to pieces.

The State Attorney, Ira Dubuskey, was hot. He was a sharpshooter from the Special Prosecution Division. He even went so far as to take Gregg to another court and get immunity from prosecution granted for him. But Gregg still wouldn't talk and when the D.A. started screaming about how Gregg's afraid for his life and that's why he won't talk, Judge Carling Stedman said he agreed with him. He said he thought the guy probably was afraid for his life and he, Judge Stedman, wasn't going to force Gregg to risk his life by demanding that he talk.

My lawyer was a guy by the name of Leonard Moriber. Lenny was a stand up guy and plenty of guts. The Judge was always threatening to hold him in contempt and for sure he didn't get pushed around in court.

That was just the first of what was to be a whole string of trips back and forth to Miami that first year as my appeals were heard and new charges were filed against me.

I was to lose all of the appeals but none of the new charges were to stick.

While we were watching the Gregg case fall apart, I was still putting my hopes on getting a medium-custody classification, being moved into the "O" Unit and then shipped out to some medium or minimum security prison.

While in the Dade County Jail I got word that the $1,500 had been sent to Oliver. It was a suckers play. He let them send a money order to his house, made out to him. When I found out how they'd asked to have the money delivered, I thought, "This guy's going to get busted."

After the Gregg case was over, I had to sit around the Dade County Jail until they had another trip going up to Raiford. Finally, they had two other guys going up one day with a couple of deputies and so they sent me along with them. I was on my way back to prison again . . . but it beat the Gray Goose.

3

As we came in through the gate at Raiford, that same old feeling of hopelessness descended on me. Those closing gates were closing in on my head too, on my mind. I had to get out of there. I wondered if Oliver had done his thing yet.

It'd be just like him, his type, to get my money and do nothing. Then if I went to him and said what's going on, he'd act like he didn't know me. "Don't bother, boy," he'd say. Well, I'd bother him all right. I could cook his goose with that money order made out to him. He's just not bright, not right bright, that's his problem. Then I began to wonder if he was bright enough to get me the custody classification I wanted. Well, he'd better be. He had my $1,500 and I was tired of having a door unlocked for me every time I wanted to go in or out and a guard frisking me every time I turned around.

When the deputies turned me in, they got a receipt for me, just like I was a registered package. After they checked me in and searched me, I was assigned a bunk in the same dorm. Welcome back.

Charlie Burden, a guy I'd known on the street, came up to me as I was putting my gear in my locker.

He was a real hard hitter on the street and one of the "Good Guys." He was doing life for a robbery I was going to go on with him except for a last minute change of plans.

"How'd you do, Frank," he asked.

"Okay, I beat the rap," I answered.

"Good," he said.

"What's good about it?"

"Anytime you go to court and don't get more time, that's good, man."

"Okay. I'll buy that."

"Let's go to the canteen," he said, "I'll buy."

"Nawh, they don't have nothing in that canteen," I answered.

"Let's go to the outside canteen at The Rock," he came back, "I got it fixed." Charlie was a mover.

We weren't allowed in The Rock. We weren't allowed anywhere outside the classification area of the West Unit unless we had a hospital chit or a dentist's chit or something, or we had a trusty taking us some place, which only made going mean more because we were getting over on the hacks.

These trusties could move back and forth wherever they wanted to and they just about ran the prison. If you had money, you could do just about anything you wanted to do, get just about anything you wanted to get. I had already been in the outside canteen at The Rock a couple of times . . . I'd gotten a slip for the hospital signed by Oliver or Cotton had gotten for me. Then I'd gotten a trusty to stop by the canteen with me.

The same way, I had gotten permission to wear my own civilian shoes . . . it took a note from the doctor saying my feet wouldn't "adjust" to prison boots. A trusty handled it all. The same way with the dentist. The guy who made the appointment was a trusty. If you had money you could get on the waiting list and see the dentist. If you didn't, your name would get on the list, but it would always be bumped down the line by guys who were taking care of the trusty.

The outside canteen at The Rock also served as a lunch room for the guards and the canteen for the visitor's park. You've got to have eaten a lot of institutional food to understand the appeal that particular canteen had for us. It wasn't just that the food in that canteen wasn't gray in either color or taste, it was that it was like free-world food. Part of my sentence, in a way, was to eat institutional food for twenty-two and a half years, too, and getting to eat in that canteen beat the state out of that part of our sentences.

They really had the food in there. You could get stuff like spaghetti and meatballs with oregano and real parmesan cheese and hamburgers with all the trimmings. They even had milkshakes in there. Really good food.

"I got blank, signed chits, man," Charlie said. "I also got the Speedball," he was talking about Henry Cotton, "to walk us over there." Charlie didn't like Cotton, because he was a speed freak, but out we went and met him and another guy they called Squid and they took us to the outside canteen. When we got inside, they went to talk to some other guys and we got in the line.

When there were only about three guys left in front of Charlie some guy tried to edge in front of me, between Charlie and me, and I gave him a short jab in the ribs that sent him over to lean against the wall. Turkey! Who did he think I was, huh?

One thing I had already learned in the joint, just the little time I had been there. You had to establish who you were, quick, if you didn't want people trying to walk all over you. I knew nobody was going to walk on me but I also didn't even want them trying me out. Now I had a reputation that came into prison ahead of me. A lot of the guys in here had known me on the street. I knew word had gone around the West Unit that though I was in for burglary I was also a hit man and a hard hitter on the street.

Still, I knew you had to establish your sincerity in this place. Lots of guys came in with a reputation for being real macho outside who turned out to be not all that tough.

Well, if Oliver tried to cut me out, man, I'd establish my sincerity in this place, fast.

There was always some game going down. Some dude trying to get over on someone else.

Just as Charlie and I got in the line, this dude comes up and says, "Give me a cigarette."

It's not a question.

I said, "I don't have nothing for you."

He said, "Give me a smoke man," and started reaching for my pocket.

I stabbed him. No problems, no discussion, no nothing. He didn't get his smoke, he got a belly full of steel. I didn't kill him, I didn't even try to kill him, but he sure hurt.

Speedball was bent out of shape. He was really scared. By the time the guards got in there, none of us had done it and the garbage can held whatever anyone was carrying. The guy that got stuck didn't know how it happened, he said. At least he wasn't a rat. But now, for sure, an enemy.

We left with Speedball nervously hurrying us along. He yakked all the way back to the dorm about not doing him right.

Charlie and I didn't go to chow that night. We just laid on our bunks talking about Miami and who was doing what. The F.B.I. was still looking for Fredie Yokum. What a wildman. Not even 21 and on the "10 most wanted list." We heard stories about a shoot-out with the Feds in Atlanta but didn't know how much was true.

Jack Murphy and Jack Griffith got busted for the Whiskey Creek murders. That didn't seem like Jack's style, but he was in *Big Trouble.*

It seems one of his partners called "The Cat" or something had turned sour and it looked like we'd be seeing them anyday now.

My partner Dominic Bretti lost his appeal and was on his way up with a 35-year bit. His appeal looked strong. The heat in Dade County must have had something to do with it.

We talk a little more about Dade County — about the "Killer Squad" headed by Capt. Longbottom — about how the sheriff, Tal Buchanan, got busted with a bunch of key deputies, and the general clean-up campaign they were having . . . things were hot. While we were talking I became aware of these guys down at the end of the dorm. Everybody else had gone to chow but there were five or six guys down there standing around a bunk, jazzing some guy who was apparently trying to take a nap.

I looked to see who he was and he was a kid I remembered. He had been on the Gray Goose with me when we came up from Miami. A good looking kid, blond, well built, the kind of guy you see performing for the women on the beach. A beach boy.

It was a warm afternoon and he was stretched out just in his skivvies. The guys standing around his bed were looking at him. I could hear them easily.

"Hey, pretty boy," one cooed at him.

Another said, "What you got there, pretty boy?"

Each remark fell with a splash, like the huge raindrops that come at the beginning of a bad storm.

"Look at that muscle," another said.

And another chuckled, "Look at that pretty flesh."

"Soft flesh," another said. They all picked up on it. Symphonic.

"Pretty flesh."

"Nice Muscle."

"Warm skin."

"Blonde hair."

"Legs flare."

"Come fair."

"Let's pair."

"He's got a pair."

"I'll take mine rare."

"I want my share."

The tempo of their remarks had lifted into a rhythm and they would lean forward as they spoke and then rock back and they were swaying and bobbing and three or four were speaking at once . . . short staccato sentences or phrases. The tension was building.

"Hey, man, you're mine."

"I like your butt mighty fine."

"We gonna have you on the line."

"When you're ready give a sign."

And the rhythm changed.

"Pretty meat."

"Can't be beat."

"Keep your seat."

"Ain't he neat."

"Tickle them feet."

They were moving around his bunk now, weaving as they went, almost chanting . . . and I began to know what they planned to do.

Suddenly the blonde youth sat up and yelled at them. "Get out here, you guys, I ain't done nothing to you."

It was a mistake, his voice was shrill and fear-filled. The first one reached out and touched him, gently, just wiping his palm up his forehead and over his wavy blonde hair, saying, "You have what we want, buddyboy, you're going to do something for us now."

I turned to Charlie and said, "If that guy resists, if he tries to fight them instead of getting raped, let's just go ahead and get on these guys."

"I'm with you," Charlie said.

But the kid didn't fight, he just laid back flat on the mattress, staring at them.

"Yeah, man, we're going to let you help us now."

"Yeah, man, I need a lot of help, fast, man."

"Yeah, man I'm going to let you help yourself, man."

"Yeah, man, I've got something for you, man."

"You're ours boy, it's time to get right or die, make love or die."

"You want to keep that deep voice, man, you better help me with my big problem."

"Big problem." They all echoed it, setting up a rhythm with it and tossing the three syllables back and forth, up and down. They wove around his bunk in a grotesque threat to the young boy who was pushing himself deeper into the flat mattress. He had pulled the pillow from under his head and had it clutched tightly across his chest.

"Big problem!"
"Big problem!"
"Big problem!"
"Big problem!"

They began to peel their pants open and bobbing and swaying, singing "your ours" to the almost mesmerized youth, they began to push in on him.

"Touch me man," one of them said.

I said, "Charlie, let's get out of here."

"Let's go."

On the way out of the dorm, I said to him, "I wish one of those characters would try that with me." I was really hot.

Charlie answered, very casually, "You don't have to worry about that. You're just like them, they won't bother you."

It was like somebody hit me with a baseball bat.

"Hold on," I said, turning to him. "I'm not like them! I never raped anybody, let alone rape any boy. What are you talking about, I'm like them?"

"I never said you raped any boy, Frank, I just said they won't touch you because you're like them. You're a taker, you take whatever you want. You always have."

That stopped me. We moved on toward the door.

As we went through the doorway, I could hear the kid pleading with them, "Don't hurt me, you guys, don't hurt me. I'll do what ever you want, just don't hurt me." He screamed just once, and then the scream was muffled with his pillow.

Outside the door, I turned to Charlie again. "So."

"Those guys are victims, too, Frank. They haven't had no lovin' in years, some of them. They want to feel their flesh on flesh, even if it's a man's and they have to imagine it's a woman's. It's better than no flesh at all. They're as much a victim of who they are as the kid is."

"You ain't served no time, yet, Frank," he went on, "You don't know it but it's a lonely place here. You ain't never been lonely in your life 'til you've built some time in a prison like this. It's a lonesomeness that eats at you day and night. Some of it comes from the people who don't ever write you, some of it comes from the way the guards talk to you, like you're a nothin', dirt under their feet, like you'll never be good enough for people out there to mess with again." He waved his hand out toward the darkness beyond the fences, toward the "free world."

"Some of it comes from the cold walls and the iron doors . . . like outside, you can always think tomorrow will be better when you're feeling low, but not in here. In here you know tomorrow ain't goin' to hold nothin' today didn't hold. The people are going to be the same, the time you have to build is going to be the same, the guards are going to be the same . . . and the loneliness creeps up on you like the cold does in a room where the fire's gone out."

I wasn't even hearing him anymore and he turned away from me and joined a group of men standing in the yard.

"You're just like them, Frank." The words echoed in my head, reverberating like a voice does in an empty gym, drifting away,then coming back.

"You're one of them. A taker . . . "

Hell yes, I'm a taker, I thought. The givers are losers. If you don't take, you end up getting screwed, just like that kid in there. The givers are the weak ones. I'm a taker and I'm proud of it!

My thoughts were broken by Charlie calling out

to me through the darkness.

"Come on Frank," he said, "we got a poker game coming together. Let's go."

I went.

That night, though, when I laid my head on the pillow to go to sleep, the words came back. "You're just like them Frank. You're a taker. You always take whatever you want."

4

When I woke up the next morning, I had an uneasy feeling that comes from your subconscious mind when things aren't just right. I brushed it aside.

I shut it out and made plans to go and find Cotton. I hadn't been able to say anything the day before because we never were alone. When I got over to classification and found him, I asked him, "Does Oliver acknowledge receipt of the money?"

"Yeah," he said, "He got it okay. Everything's set."

"That's fine," I said, "What do we do next?"

"We don't do anything, we just wait now. Trust me, it's all taken care of. We've got Oliver in the bag, man."

"I can wait, man."

"You know," he said, "I've been able to get little things from Oliver before, you know, a phone call, kite out a letter, little miscellaneous things here and there . . . but this is the first time I ever got him to really bite the bait for a straight-out bribe."

"What you're telling me is you're moving up on him, huh, man?"

"What I'm telling you is we ain't no longer guard an prisoner, man, we're partners now and we're going to see some changes around here now."

Oliver didn't belong to himself anymore. He was now our man in the prison . Everything was cool.

The fish was hooked. When I was in the "O" Unit, Oliver would become the victim. We own him.

"I'm ready, man." I sent back to my dorm thinking about a job outside the fence somewhere . . .

A couple weeks went by, then suddenly one afternoon I was told to get all of my stuff together. I was being transferred.

"Where to ?" I asked.

"You'll find out when you get there," the guard answered, "get down to the classification office." Frustration, like a hand on my throat, gripped me. The way these guys talk to you make you want to cut their hearts out. Hate welled up inside me but I kept it hidden and thought of someday . . . someday.

Turning away from the guard, I went to pack my gear. On my way back from the dorm, I saw Henry Cotton moving across the yard toward me. He looked up, saw me, then glanced aside and turned his head away toward one of the other dorms.

I thought,"Something's wrong here. What's up?" I tried to figure what he was up to. Suspicion bristled around me. Then I thought, "Maybe somebody's watching us." I put my stuff down, as if to shift the load, and as I did I turned and sure enough, there was a guard coming across the yard just behind me. I waited until he had gone past me, then shouldered my gear again and started toward the classification office.

By this time Cotton was almost opposite me and as he went past me, he turned toward me and raised his hand with a thumb-and-forefinger okay sign, nodded his head just a hair and winked at me.

Okay, man, okay. So they had done it. Okay, this was more like it.

Other guys were coming into the office with their stuff and a guard was lining everybody up.

"Okay, boys," he said. "As I call your name, answer with your number and then step forward and I'll tell you where you're going.

"East Unit and "O" Unit guys who are going to The Rock, go through that door and wait in there until you're called," and he pointed to a door at one side of the room.

There were guards on both sides of the gate and through the gate we could see a prison van parked with more guards standing between the building and the van.

"Adams, Kenneth," the guard called out.

"20961," came the answer as a young guy stepped forward.

"East Unit," said one guard, motioning toward the gate. That was maximum security and I wondered what the kid had done. They only sent the worst offenders or fags to the East Unit. You can't really tell much about a guy the way he looks.

Without a pause the young man slung the bag on his shoulder and as he moved toward the gate, the locks slammed open, the guard pushed the gate back, he walked through and the gate was slammed behind him again as the locks clacked back into place.

"Atwood, "Curtis," the guard called.

"20978," an older man, hair almost white, said as he stepped forward.

"East Unit," the guard said and the man moved through the gate.

"Branch, Daniel," the guard called.

"In the van, "O" Unit." the guard said.

I wondered what he had done to make the "O"

Unit as he went through the gate.

"Costantino, Frank," the guard called.

I took a step forward, said, "20952" and then moved off toward the gate.

"Where do you think you're going?" The guard's voice was shrill.

"Did I tell you where to go ?" I stopped.

Then, getting his voice under control, he called out, in a voice now identical to the earlier calls, "The Rock."

The Rock! Close security! What had happened? Prepared as I was to step off again toward the gate, I had to pause a moment before I could step off in the right direction. Iron control kept me from stumbling or making an awkward movement which would reveal the violent anger I felt.

My face a blank mask, I moved through the door, anger and frustration boiling up inside of me.

So, Henry Cotton had given me the okay sign, huh? We had Oliver in the bag, did we??? My time would come, my time would come. Cotton was probably going to get himself fixed up when he gave me the high sign. Junkie! Well, I could take care of him. I didn't need any help for that. Junkie!

Later they walked us over into the Rock and I walked there in a cloud of revenge. They didn't tell us anything when we got there, just sent us to skid row with the rest of the guys. Later on, I found it was an 18 man cell for unassigned inmates, "transients," they called us. There were all kinds of guys up there. Some of them like us, just coming in and others going out, mostly to other prisons.

I sat on my bunk planning what I was going to do to Henry Cotton, but as I was going to sleep that night, some guys began horsing around with young

Alvarez, in his bunk, and I got that sick feeling inside that we were going to have another rape.

Then, suddenly, Alvarez jumped up, a knee in a guy's crotch and the dude went down. Alvarez did a show number on his head, I mean he kicked the hell right out of him. A big guy from the other side of the room put his hand on his shoulder and kind of patted him, then stood up and faced the other guys.

"You want something out of Juan," he said, "you better think about it."

Juan had heart. Good for him, he'd make it.

Relieved, I rolled over and shut my eyes and as my head sank into the pillows, I thought of two kinds of people, those who take and those who get taken. Juan wasn't just like them, but he was a taker. He had the heart to do what he had to do.

"You're a taker, Frank, you always take whatever you want."

The sound of the words, like waves, rose and fell within my being.

The next morning somebody saved Cotton's life . . . and Oliver's. I went over to classification with everyone else to find out what kind of work assignment I would have in the Rock.

I was angry and while everybody else was thinking about what they'd be doing while they were building their time, I was thinking about the "O" Unit and how I'd been double crossed. However, when I went before the classification team, instead of hearing them give me a job assignment, I heard the classification officer say to them, "No, you don't need to give him a job assignment. He's classified for the "O" Unit."

Okay! Okay! This is more like it. Something of my old self began to course through my body as I got my gear and got on the van for the trip across to the "O" Unit.

When the van dropped me off, the first guy I looked up was a trusty who had been referred to me. We talked a little about the incident in the Rock and the pro's and con's of this joint. With him going through the who was a rat, who was a punk, routine . . .

We talked about that some and I arranged to get another knife. I began to create a "place" for myself in the "O" Unit, in the days that followed and in the kitchen where I had been assigned to work.

I watched what was coming down and who was into what. It's wise to find out who feels they have what, and where their heads are.

I wasn't interested in any of the convict games, or happenings. Some of the guys approached me because of my street reputation, and some light friendship developed. Nothing heavy. I was into an escape, nothing more and I didn't want to bring down any heat. I knew the system and was trying to use it to my best advantage. Just get along. Some of the hacks thought I was a live one.

"Hey Frank," one of them would say, "What's happening down on 'E' wing? Little beef down there, last night?" They knew there was a beef. They broke it up. I dumbied up. "I don't know," I said, "I hit the sack early."

Well, I wasn't their stoolie and I didn't have any rap for him. Just dummy up. Don't ever let the man know you're hip to his cop games, that could cause a lot of grief.

My room turned out to be just like Cotton had said. The "O" Unit was star shaped, one story, and there were about 30 cells in each arm, 15 on each side of a central corridor running the length of the arm. There were bars on the corridor end.

As I entered it, there was a sliding barred door on the left front side of the cell. On the right was a double bunk that ran from the bars back to a wall at the back of the cell. There was a door in the center of that wall and behind the wall was a shower on the right and a john and basin on the left. In the middle of the wall behind it was another door and it led to the "sun room" a room with no windows, but the top was open to the sky except for criss-crossed bars.

Opposite the bunks was a double locker and two chairs. I had been in lots worse places. My roommate was a quiet little guy, I don't think he said ten words to me the whole time we shared that cell. At first I thought he was afraid of me, but later on I learned he didn't talk much to anybody.

As cells went, it was a good cell and you couldn't beat having a private bath. I remember one time I was in jail in Massachusetts and you didn't have any plumbing in your cell. You had a little bucket to use, and I mean it was little. There was a knack to using it, but I just never got the hang of it. Anyway, first thing every morning, they came along and unlocked your cell before breakfast and you had to take your bucket, they called them "honey-buckets," and go down the hall to this big cistern and dump it and wash it out, then take it back to your cell. After that you could go eat your breakfast if you wanted to.

That night, the trusty I had first met when I got off the van that day brought me a new shank. I gave him a carton of smokes. I think every inmate in Raiford was well heeled. They all had knives. The place was a regular blood-bath. The only people in the place who weren't armed were the guards. A dozen or so inmates got killed every year. More than two hundred of them got stabbed.

The work in the kitchen was easy and the way the shifts were run, I had plenty of time. We could come and go as we pleased and they didn't lock us up 'til ten at night.

The weeks began to turn into months.

5

Now that I was settled, most of my time was taken up with my thoughts of escape. That was the reason I had bought the custody reduction. I had plenty of time to think about it, in the kitchen and in my cell. On occasion the thought "You're just like them, Frank. You take what you want," would flash through my mind.

I tried to shove the thought out of my mind but it kept coming back. Then I'd argue with the thought. I'd say to myself, Nawh! That's not right. I'm not like them. I'd say to myself. I'm a taker but I'm not like them.

And that other me inside of me was saying, *yes you are, it's the same . . . those guys raping that kid were taking what they wanted just because they wanted it and they didn't care who they hurt in the process.*

It's not the same . . . they were raping that guy. Rape is not the same as robbery. I never raped anybody . . . I was just doing what I had to do.

I caught a glimpse of myself. Just a small glimpse but a glimpse none-the-less. I slammed my mind shut against it and said to myself . . . No. That's not me. Oh, no, no, no, NO!

I couldn't keep it out of my mind. I had a glimpse at who I really was. All the baloney, all the cool, all the glamour stripped away. I couldn't understand it. I didn't know where these thoughts were coming from. I'd never had thoughts like these before. Why now? Why here, of all places?

That voice within me, where was it coming from?

Why was it haunting me? Ringing in my ears and clinging to my heart.

I've always done what I thought was right. I've never shorted anybody on a deal. I could be trusted. I never ratted anyone out no matter what. Hadn't those two Feds down at the Dade County Jail offered me out on this 22½ years, plus other benefits, if I would, in their lingo, wise up and cooperate? That's not my style.

I've never taken something that wasn't my share. I've handled a lot of swag and you won't find anybody who was ever in on a deal with me saying I cheated on him.

You take it because you want it, Frank.

There's lots of things I want I don't take. I want all the swag we take in a robbery but I don't take it. I always split just the way we agreed. I had a code I lived by and I had heart. I always did what I had to do.

You're a taker, Frank. You don't care about people, about what happens.

Maybe so, but I have honor, I do the right things, life is a jungle where only the strong survive.

. . . and the robberies I'd committed began to walk back into my mind and they'd just stand there . . . and stare at me . . . and some of them would be people who were involved and some of them wouldn't be people, they'd be things, like a building and it'd have eyes, eyes that followed you no matter which way you walked around it . . . and all the eyes would glare at me, unblinking . . . and the diamonds, the diamonds had hundreds of eyes, thousands of eyes, they all blinked at me, looking at me, each blink saying, "I've seen you at work, Frank."

Once I woke in the middle of the night, and found I was dreaming of paying the fiddler. I was being treated just like I had treated others. I was cold with fear . . . what in the world is happening to me?

I knew at that moment if I was going to be treated the way I had treated others, I was in a hard place. "No I shouted, dammit, no, I won't let you." My victims wanted *justice*.

In that half-way place between being asleep and awake, I realized I had spoken aloud, I continued to argue silently with them as they faded into consciousness . . . I wasn't any worse than a lot of people. The world is full of takers, it's just the way things are if you're poor.

As I argued, awakening, the eyes retreated further and further and then one of the last glimmers fluttered up briefly and this faint voice said, "What about me, what did I ever do to you?" Pain swept through me as I faced an accuser I couldn't answer.

. . . and that other voice in me said, "See, you don't care *who you hurt, Frank*."

"I didn't . . ." I began and suddenly realized I was speaking aloud again. I gritted my teeth and struggled against the conflict waging in my thoughts.

I've got a reason for the things I do! I've got a reason for behaving the way I behave.

I began to give myself the reasons. I couldn't get a good job like other people did because of that bad conduct discharge from the Navy. They had fixed it so I couldn't work like other people. I'd grown up in a house with a couple of alcoholics and I'd learned you couldn't depend on what people said. The only person you could depend on was yourself. I'd been hungry sometimes when I was a kid and I had this fear of being hungry. I'd dream about there not being anything, anywhere, to eat.

Hadn't that guy in that book I read said what I did probably wasn't my fault anyway? Maybe he was right, after all. Life sure hadn't been any bed of roses when I was a kid.

When I tried to remember what it was like as a kid, I couldn't remember a whole lot. I didn't have any mother. Well, of course, I had had a mother but I didn't remember her. I had a sister too, but she had left with my mother so I couldn't remember her either. My dad never mentioned her so I was in the Navy before I knew she existed. I can remember living alone with my little brother, Robert, and my dad.

We didn't see a whole lot of my dad. Way back then, I already knew he drank a lot. I also knew that his bottle of beer was more important to him than I was.

Then one day he took us up to another town in Massachusetts and put us in an orphanage. I guess he just didn't want to be bothered with us anymore, who knows.

That orphanage was a bad scene. I guess they were good people there trying to help the kids but what came across was that nobody really loved you, they just cared for you. We didn't always have enough to eat and since everything seemed to be based on how long you'd been there, we started at the bottom of the ladder in everything.

My brother and I were separated. I got put at the last table in the dining room and I got the last chair at the table which meant that everything got passed to me last. I stayed hungry. Our table was the last one allowed to go up to get our platters and sometimes there wasn't much left when we got up there.

So, I learned to steal food. I finally got to where I could palm a piece of bacon (when we had any) with the cook looking right at me when I took a platter from the stove to put it on the serving counter.

As soon as breakfast was over on weekdays we went to school. That was better. Except the other kids teasing you because you were an orphan. I'd tell them I wasn't, that my father and my mother were both alive but they wouldn't believe me . . . .and some of them would say "no, they weren't alive," and sometimes at night in the bed by the door with the cold blowing through the cracks, I'd wake up and I wouldn't believe it either.

After school we had chores to do. The same thing every day. It didn't make any difference at all to them what you wanted to do, they'd just beat your butt if you didn't do it. You learned to do what you had to do to survive.

Night time was the best and worst time of the day. After we had eaten we could go outside and play, summer or winter. I didn't get on any teams for a long time because the guys already had teams and then too, they'd say I was too young. Anyway, it was still fun because you could almost always find someone to pitch a ball with and there were some games, like tag, that didn't have any teams. It was free time.

Then back to your room and study and then get

ready for bed. It was lonely.

They kept telling us we had to be grateful. I got sick with the measles and they put me in a room by myself and left me there in the dark with the shades drawn all day long until I was over them. I didn't have anybody to talk to or anything and when the nurse came by each morning and each night, all she'd tell me was how grateful I should be.

If I tried to tell her how lonesome I was or anything, she'd tell me all about how there were some kids in Boston no older than I was who didn't have any place at all to stay. How they lived on the streets and maybe slept in a cardboard box behind a building or something and didn't have anything to eat except what they could get out of garbage cans or steal . . . and so I should be very grateful.

Pretty soon I outgrew the clothes my dad had brought with me. They took those clothes away from me and gave them to somebody else. Then they gave me some clothes that another guy had outgrown. A lot of them had patches and seams which had been sewn back together over and over . . . and I should be grateful?

I was hungry, ragged and cold and I should be grateful? I wanted to run away but I didn't know where to run to. Two years later my dad came back, took us to New York and introduced us to a new mother. The four of us went to Miami to live.

So, maybe it all wasn't my fault. That's what that guy in the book had said. He said, "You have behaved in a way that has been anti-social because your environments were sub-normal in one way or another and you developed amorphous behavior patterns."

I remember what he said because I didn't

understand the word "amorphous," so I went to the library and looked it up. The dictionary said it meant "having no determinate form."

Then he said, "Behavior patterns, however, can be modified and that is what is done to prisoners during their period of incarceration."

Well, I knew one thing. I was angry and full of hate and resentment. I sure wasn't going to do anything that was *their way*.

Some guard would tell you to do something, something you knew wouldn't work, or worse, and you'd try to tell the dumb jerk it wouldn't work, knowing you knew ten times as much as he did about anything and when you tried to tell him he was wrong, that was it. If you weren't careful, you'd find yourself locked up for 10 days, 20 days, 30 days. Well, at least I hadn't had to learn that here. I'd learned that in Portsmouth Naval Prison when I was in the Navy.

That's the way the Navy "modified" your behavior. They'd just put you away in that dark little box all by yourself and leave you there for days and days and days in the dark. In a place where there isn't any "behaving" to do, so of course it "modified your behavior." I spent 14 days in the box at Newport. At first you spend most of your time thinking about food because you're so hungry or about a cigarette or being hot or cold or the smell. Pretty soon you're doing things to try to keep from flipping. Then you start hating, it's the hating that works. It's the hating that keeps you from flipping.

Night after night I would lay on the mattress on the floor of that tiny box in that Navy prison and fantasize about what I would do to that chaser who was responsible for me being put in that hole. I began to be eaten up alive by the hatred. It was like a cancer.

A day is really long when you're locked up in a dark cell with no furniture, no toilet, just a hole in the floor with running water and total darkness. Time drags by hard.

I'd had my share of hard times back in those Navy days and I wasn't going to be a chump here, so I laid low and didn't make waves. You could fight them if you wanted to but it's a no-win situation. No right, no wrong.

You could beat them in little things and some guys spent every waking hour trying to figure up ways to beat the system. Sometimes they'd come up with things that would give them a brief sense of being "in control." Crazy things.

To some it was the only way they could keep the hate inside them from driving them mad. Small victories. Things that would seem petty on the outside.

Like the time Fat Dog robbed the canteen hack for the canteen books. It was only a couple of hundred bucks in prison script but it was the Raiford score of the year.

"Dog" grinned like a cat for a week and I don't think he could even spend the books.

That guard wasn't breaking bad when Fat Dog had a knife at his throat, he was copping deuces. Everybody in the joint loved it.

Or the guy who was working on the cowboys' squad from the "O" Unit and rustling state cows and selling them to the local buyers while he was still doing time. To add insult to injury he escaped on a state horse before they busted him. Great stuff for morale.

I don't care how bright you are, when you first come into the prison system, you have a kind of illusion of immunity about yourself. You think the things that are happening can't happen to you. As time rolls on, however, you realize it can happen to you and the hate can become manifested. Soon the games become important to you, for survival if nothing else.

I had gotten through Portsmouth but that was only a six-month bit. Here I was building twenty-two and a half years.

I was becoming frustrated with the increasing realization that I was reacting to the system . . . that the hate and the desire to beat the system, to get the best of them, was a temptation I wasn't resisting. I was that way in the box at Portsmouth.

Inside I was screaming at them, "Don't you know you can't do this to me? Nobody, but nobody treats me this way!"

But there wasn't anybody outside that box to hear you, even if you screamed it out loud.

There wasn't anybody in this place to hear it either. Nobody to hear the anger, the loneliness, the frustration. If you yelled it at them they'd just hear the words. Nothing more.

I learned real quick the prison concept of behavior modification. Immediate punishment for things that are wrong, and vague promises of reward (parole) for things that are right. Behave and you'll get out before your entire sentence is served. Don't behave and you'll think you've served five sentences before your time is out and you'll serve everyday the judge gave you.

Kind of like the same principles we raise our kids by.

"No, no, Johnny!" Slap! Slap!

"Yes, yes, Johnny. Good! Good!" Pat, pat.

But they aren't.

With our kids, the pat-pat is delivered with love.

In prison, the pat-pat is delivered grudgingly, distrustfully and only when there is no other choice.

I came to see, quickly, that the entire system operated as a pushing of authority out of fear, a fear of punishment, of more degradation. It doesn't have to be a fear of physical danger. It is done with fear of what they can do to you against your will, so they modify your free will and your behavior because they are stronger than you are.

That very rapidly becomes a case of some guards saying, "I'm right because I'm stronger than you are." So the old phrase, "Might makes right," becomes true in prison. The guy who doesn't learn it doesn't see much daylight.

It's only natural that kind of power begins to be corrupted and as the days went by and I moved around the prison I saw the corruption all around me. I thought of that phrase about "power corrupts, absolute power corrupts absolutely." Guards and sometimes trusties were caught up in distorted concepts of who they were. In a very real sense they too were victims of who they were and the experiences they encountered. Only now they had the upper hand.

Then one day I realized that's what those guys were doing that day when they raped that kid. They did it because that's what they wanted to do and there were five of them, or six, or whatever, and so they were the strong. The kid was only one, and a very weak one. They did it, just like the guards were doing to us, regardless of the way the kid felt because that's what they wanted to do.

Then, in a flash . . . it was like, did you ever see a window shade when the spring popped? Nobody's around it, it just suddenly shoots up and reveals everything that's outside it? Or if you're outside looking in, inside it? Well, just that suddenly I saw that I was just like that. There wasn't a bit of difference between the prison's treatment of the prisoner, or the rapists' treatment of that kid and Frank's treatment of people all of his life.

The minute I recognized that, I tried to pull the shade down again. I said no. No way. I'm not like that! It's not true! But that me, deep within me said, "Frank, there's really no difference in your behavior and the rapists' behavior. There's no difference between the guard's action toward you and your action toward everybody you've ever known."

I was still trying to pull the shade down on what I had seen but the voice kept on . . .

You've always wanted power over the people around you, Frank. When you were a kid, you wanted power over the other kids around you and resented the fact that they were mostly bigger than you were.

I did what I had to do. I wanted more power in the orphanage to protect Bobby. The same way when we got to Miami.

It was because you had to be in control, Frank. As you grew up you had to have power over the guys you ran with and pretty soon it was over everybody around you.

I had to look out after myself.

That's right, you didn't get into situations where you didn't have power over everybody else.

Somebody's got to be boss. You can't have all

indians and no chiefs.

You're just like the guards, you're just like those guys raping that kid. How does it feel, now it's happening to you? You're on the other end of the stick now, Frank, it's happening to you now . . .

Like a tree suddenly illuminated in the darkness by a bolt of lightning, I saw how the guy who was abused felt and I was able to identify with him. I could see the unfairness of the strong man, the abuser. I could identify as the abuser in my lifestyle . . . not only in the past but in my lifestyle right at the moment in prison.

The voice came back again, *Frank, your entire life, even here in prison, has dealt with the intimidation of people. You've either done it by hurting them or by the implied threat of injury.*

. . . and I knew that was the way I had been, the way I was . . . but I also knew there was a reason for it. My environment had done it. That's what that book had said. It wasn't my fault, it was my environment.

Everytime I would be wandering around in my memory and come across a time I'd hurt somebody, find it sitting there waiting for me, saying . . .

Look, Frank, this is what you're like.

I'd say to myself, "No, no, it's not. I'm not really like that."

It was the things that happened to me, the pressures around me. I didn't have any control over what made me do that. When I would say that, the thought, the accusation, would go away . . . for an hour or a day.

. . . but it always came back. *You're just like them, Frank. You don't care, you're a taker . . . and takers are losers . . .*

I knew it was true and hate began to grow in me, hate toward everything in everybody I didn't like in myself.

I hadn't ever liked those guys who had been in on the rape but now I began to hate them. I never saw any of them unless I went over to the Rock for something, but everytime I thought of them I hated them and I hated them more and more everyday because they made me see a me I didn't really like.

I began to have periods of great despair, of hopelessness, especially when I was working on some stupid job all alone. Sometimes I couldn't believe it. I wasn't anything! A number, that's what I was, a number. You couldn't tell there was any difference from me and any other guy in the joint. I had the same clothes. I had the same address, the same bunk, the same blanket.

I might as well be a machine or a power tool or a switchboard. What difference was there between them and me? I had feelings, that was all, and who knows, maybe a machine has feelings too.

I was peeling turnips in the kitchen one day and I got to thinking, I wonder what in the world this turnip thinks about being peeled and thrown in the pot?

There was a big fat turnip right on top of the bunch and I snatched him up and held him out at arm's length, the tail of the root forming a single, wispy hair from his pointed head, the few greens on the trimmed stems making ragged pants for him.

"Aha!" I said, "You know what I'm going to do with you? I'm going to cut your head off." With a slash of the knife right above where my fist grasped his body, I lopped off his head. Then I said, "Now,

I'm going to cut your feet off." And whoosh, it was done.

Then I said, "Now, I'm going to skin you alive!"

I wondered what that turnip felt about it all . . . and I was inspired that day and I went back to my cell and I wrote a poem. For the first time in my life, I was inspired and I went and wrote a poem and the name of the poem was "The Turnip's Point of View." I can still remember it . . .

I was born of two sexes,
My cradle was the earth
My gentle mother, Nature,
Gave me life blood after birth
To take and draw on freely
For my needs she knew
In the comfort of her love for me
I thrived and grew.
Then parting fate appeared
As it sometimes does
And ripped me cruelly
From the bosom of earth's love,
And cast me with the masses
In misery and despair.
And though many more are with me
I am not their care
Because we wait alone, together,
Unjustly so it seems.
Death's around the corner.
No hopes for me, no dreams.
Just the sharpened blade of destruction
Is to be my fare
And I'm going to die
A lonely turnip,
Saddened more
Because no one cares.

And I didn't care. I didn't care if I lived. I didn't care if I died, because I had finally seen who I was.

I started looking for answers.

I was looking because I was desperate.

I was looking because I was empty.

I was looking because I was hurting.

I had gotten to the end of myself and I didn't know where to go.

I was hurting and I started looking for answers.

Life was too vast for me to conceive with my finite mind. I saw that everyone was, in some sense, captive to their own personality . . . and motivated by forces beyond their control.

One thing seemed apparent above all . . . takers are losers and people who don't care leave holes in time.

6

"In your cells, in your cells boys," the guard yelled. It was the same tone of voice he would have used for performing monkeys or cattle or dogs. The resentment surged up in me again as I moved to my cell. Ten o'clock at night and we're going to get locked up for the rest of the night.

Another night, with nothing to do except lay in the bunk and stare at the ceiling, bathed in that ever-shining light from the corridor that shone right on the bunk all night long. Shone on your face all night long so they could see if you were in your cell when they checked.

I stretched out on the bunk and right away a stream of things which I couldn't do began to flow through my mind . . . it was the same every night, the search for something that I could do to pass the time until I would fall asleep.

As my sense of identity was decreased, by so much did I feel violated as a man, as a human being. I used to think my trouble lay in having been caught, not having enough money to get the right lawyers . . . but it wasn't just that, it was something deeper. I didn't want to look inside myself but I knew it was something I had to do. I knew I had to look . . .

I didn't like what I saw. I came, for the first time in my life to see a need for law enforcement. Somehow, people's inside beings were more important than anything else. People shouldn't be able to violate them just because they were in "control." I saw a need for order in the world, for law and for order.

I was able to see, in the homosexual rape of that kid, how people would act toward other people if there were no constraints put on them.

I began to see that prison displayed examples of all of the most severe problems in society . . . all its dirt, corruption and lawlessness. The people who populated the prison were the people who created a lot of those problems.

Locking them up certainly didn't do anything about the problems. It just made it more concentrated. True, the free-world people had removed the problem-people from their midst but they hadn't solved the problems. The problems would come back some day.

. . . and that me inside of me was speaking again, saying, *Yeah, Frank, and you, you are part of the problem.*

I wondered what part as I looked for the answers. I didn't know. I was an unknown quality, even to myself. All I knew was that I had to come to grips with who I was. I saw the things that I had done to people, how I had ripped them off and treated them like dirt. Laughing at them, at their inability to cope with a man who was holding a gun in their face, with a man who was helping himself to their hoarded money, their hoarded jewels, their hoarded gods.

For the first time in my life, I could identify with the victims who I'd robbed . . . and I knew it was wrong.

I thought of that kid those guys had raped. I saw the terrible fear that was gripping that kid . . . and for the first time in my life I was able to project my own self into a situation another guy was in, at least a little bit. I saw that it was really wrong to put people in such a situation that their wills, their desires, their feelings, their codes, were horribly violated.

My mind just bogged down at trying to cope with the feelings I might have had—if it had been me.

I thought back to the time in the Dade County Jail when I was being held without bond. This millionaire blonde, Candice Mossler, was charged with the murder of her husband. The state had a heavy case against her and her nephew Melvin Lane Powers and they had big attorneys from Texas and Florida.

I wound up with a perjury charge on that dumb case. The sheriff's department was saying that the Mossler lawyer, Harvey St. John, had hired me, through my own lawyer, Jack Nagley, to kill the informant against Powers, an informer by the name of Billy Frank Mulvey.

It didn't look good because Mulvey wound up in the same cell that I was in and they found a knife on some other rat who said I was going to use it to kill Mulvey. What a hassle. Manson Hill was the chief investigative officer and he was hot. This was a big case and a witness setting offed in the jail would have been a heavy number for him to deal with.

I was moved to another cell on another floor, charged with the beef, and this dolly gets found not guilty, when it sure looked like she was guilty to me. She had the money so she had the clout. She was able to buy the full measure of justice.

A feeling of uselessness, of powerlessness, of loneliness overwhelmed me once more. In that frustration and in the depths of that despair, I came again across the fact that none of this was my fault, that it was my environment, not me, that was responsible for my presence in prison.

I grabbed that thought as it surfaced, just as a drowning man will grab a log that pops up beside him, and hugged it to me . . . into a fitful sleep.

In the following days I began to look at the whole idea of "rehabilitation." I looked up the word in the dictionary. It said in Webster's: "to restore to a former capacity."

To restore to a former capacity?

Well, in my "former capacity" I was a hoodlum. Is that what they were going to "restore" me to?

What did it all add up to?

What was life all about?

Everybody was dishonest, one way or another. Why did most of them never get caught and put in prison for it?

Why was it us that got caught?

Why did I get caught?

Why was I thinking about all of this junk instead of thinking about how to get out of this place?

So it went. Around and around. I'd start planning an escape again. Bit by bit, piece by piece, moment by moment . . . until I'd come across a snag in the plan, an obstacle I couldn't figure a way to get around. I would find myself wondering again about why I was here.

Why did I get caught?

Why was I the kind of guy I was?

What made guys different?

I had always thought I was quite a guy. I had liked me. I was proud of the place I had carved out for myself. People looked up to me. They sought me out. It had been like that ever since I was in high school. Wasn't I captain of my high school football team? You don't get to be captain of the team if guys don't like you.

Well, you let them down, too, Frank. You quit them in middle of the season. That voice was speaking to me all of the time now, not just in the sack but in the compound, in the canteen, in the kitchen.

Yeah, I'd quit in the middle of the season, but anybody else would've too if they had to put up with what I had to put up with. Just the memory of those years made me think I was smelling beer.

Even after all of these years I didn't really like beer. It wasn't the taste of it so much as it was the smell of it. I had come to hate the smell of it before I ever got out of elementary school.

That was about the time my Dad told me my mother had died. My brother Bobby and I had been playing in the yard one Sunday morning and we wanted to go down to the next block where our gang was playing football. My step-mother, whose name was Toppy, only I called her Tipsy-Topsy, started her screaming the minute I asked my Dad about it. They were both sitting in the kitchen with the radio playing and drinking beer.

"Play, play, play. All you think about is play," she yelled. "Get in there and get your room cleaned up and clean up that back porch and pick up the trash out of that yard or I'll play you." Her voice was strident and shrill and there she sat at eleven in the morning with empty beer bottles all around her and dirty dishes still in the sink, looking dingy and vulgar in her shorts and halter.

That's all she ever wore, shorts and halter. The

minute she got home from work, into the shorts and halter, into the beer. The whole house smelled of stale beer and my Dad drank right along with her.

She was like that all of the time, yelling at us and not doing anything around the house and my Dad just let her go on and get away with it. Well, we cleaned things up some and started up the street and she came to the front door and started screeching at us again . . . I just kept walking.

Walking and thinking about how I hated Miami and hated her and hated that house with its smell of stale beer and wondering how we could get away and find our real mother up in Boston.

When we came home that afternoon, she was still drinking beer and still screeching. Some women never can ask you to do something without sounding like they had already asked you twice and you should have known to do it without being asked anyway. She was like that only she never asked you to do anything, she always *told* you.

Well, she was telling me to do the dishes now. As soon as she started in on me, I said I wasn't going to be there to do it because I was going back home to Boston to my real mother where the house didn't smell like beer and that's as far as I got. My father said, real bitter, that she wouldn't have me anyway, that she was an unfeeling woman who didn't care about anybody and only took and never gave and besides all of which she was dead anyway and had been for two or three years and it was just as well for all of us.

Though I hadn't heard her mentioned or really thought about her much for a long, long time, it was like somebody slammed a door shut right in my face and when I turned around somebody else had built a wall right across where my life was going.

We went on living, though. We went to school and we played through the summers and twice we even went to New York and Boston in the summer and I met some of my aunts and uncles and cousins, my Dad's family.

Dad never had anything good to say about my mother and even with her dead now he never mentioned her except in a negative way. When he would talk about her, my step-mother would get this silly grin on her face, like she'd just won an argument. The bitch.

I learned to stay out of the way. I didn't come home except when I had to and when I got in high school I got involved in sports and that kind of took up my time. I studied some, was in the top third of my class and I was a good student.

I didn't get into trouble, except with girls. On occasion I'd have a fight. Stuff like that. Nothing heavy. Other than that I was a pretty clean kid.

When all the wild kids gathered around down at the store where they drank beer and blew grass and smoked cigarettes, I wasn't there. I didn't hang around with the wild kids. I wasn't any goody-goody guy but I spent my time in sports and I stayed out of trouble. I was a good athlete.

By the time I was a senior at Hialeah High, I was captain of the football team but my life was really hell. Things were really bad at home. My little brother was getting into trouble and by now I knew my father and Tipsy-Topsy were both alcoholics.

Beer didn't come into the house by the bottle anymore, nor did booze. The beer came in by the keg, delivered to the door by the beer truck and the booze came in by the case. They both began drinking the minute they got home from work. My Dad usually got home before her and he would clean up the kitchen and fix supper. He wasn't such a bad egg. He wasn't mean, not cruel but his moods changed so much and so quick you never knew what it was going to be like when you came home or when you got up in the morning.

He'd promise to do all sorts of things with Bobby and me and then never do any of them. It finally got to where we didn't even believe it when he promised to do something. I mean, we didn't even get excited about the thought of it, the promise of it, anymore than if we were reading about somebody doing it in a magazine or something. It just didn't have any more to do with reality than that.

Tipsy-Topsy continued to screech at me and I was getting to the place where I couldn't take much more of that. If I said anything back to her my old man got mad and then he and I would get into it.

The way Tipsy-Topsy treated my Dad stunk and it really stung me. She never did anything around the house and finally we were cleaning the house and Dad was cooking all the meals and we were making the beds and doing everything that had to be done and it made me sick. I found myself hating her more and more because of what was happening to him.

It got to where when she would get drunk she would start to abuse him and I began to try to tell him what she was, what kind of tramp she was and how she was using him and he and I'd get into it again and again. One night we even had a fist fight. Things were becoming impossible around that house.

Bobby had been in trouble with the law and was running around with a bunch of young thugs. My father was drunk every night and he and I were always at each other's throat over Tipsy-Topsy. They were both drunk all of the time and the house reeked with the smell of stale beer. All of this was happening when I was in the middle of our football season at school. I just couldn't take any more of this any longer.

I cut school one morning, went down to the Court House in Miami and enlisted in the Navy, kissed high school goodby and went off to boot camp.

So, yeah! yeah! yeah! I let them down. I let the other guys on the team down because I quit in the middle of the season. Those guys had liked me.

Did people still like me?

I didn't like me.

Why didn't I like me?

I felt as if I were a fish on the end of a long line and somebody was playing with me. No matter which way I went, whether it was to sink myself in magazines and TV or in planning my escape or in sexual fantasies or any of the other countless ways there are of building time, I always seemed to be hauled back to myself. Back to Frank Costantino. Back to who I was and what I was and what I was like and what I wanted and where I was going.

Then one day a guy I knew upped and committed suicide. I knew the guy pretty well and couldn't figure it out. He was the last guy I'd ever have figured to just hang it up. We called him Johnny Wop. He was good looking, popular, an Italian guy. That's where the name came from.

He was a tough guy of sorts but nothing heavy. Drugs was his main thing. He had good cars, boats, whatever he wanted and women, always plenty of women.

When I heard they'd found him dead, it was hard to believe. As a matter of fact, I didn't believe it. I thought somebody had gotten to him.

He was good guy to be around. Funny. Always a good crack about anything that came up. We'd played a lot of poker and I knew him as well as anybody, I guess. What I really couldn't understand was, Why? He had it made and he was free . . . in the free world.

He never said a word about why to anybody.

He just hung it up.

Well at least he checked out with style.

I tried to analyze what I knew about him, tried to figure out why he did it. Then it dawned on me that I didn't really know the guy at all. Come to think of it, I didn't even really care that he was dead.

He had never opened up enough for me to care anymore about him than I did about the television set. Sometimes he was funny, sometimes the television was entertaining. Sometimes he was brutal and cold-blooded. So was the television.

Somehow, though, nothing he ever said or did revealed anything more about him inside himself than what went on on the television screen revealed about what was inside the tube or the cabinet.

That he was dead just meant some switches in relationships. Fifty years from now, who'd know the difference? Life wouldn't stop, other guys would take his place, they'd forget Johnny Wop . . . maybe the mother would be different . . . she'd remember. I bet she'd remember.

It didn't make any difference that he was dead. His friends would mourn a while. Then they'd forget him. He was gone. Other guys would take his place. There'd just be a change in relationships.

It'd be the same if you died, Frank.

The voice pierced me. Spiralling through my mind, it pierced every defense I had. I thought, no, no, no, it wouldn't. I'm a lot more important than he was.

To whom, Frank?

Why, to . . . to . . . and I couldn't come across a name of a person who I was sure would think my death was of any importance.

To . . . to Bunny. Yeah, to Bunny. My wife. After all, she was my wife, I had to be important to her.

How important has she been to you, Frank?

Why, very important. Sure she has, she's the best looking girl, always has been . . .

It was important to you to have a good looking wife. That's her looks Frank. It was always important to you to have a big black cadillac too. How about her, Frank? How about Bunny?

Why, she's my wife. She's the mother of my children!

What about all the other women, Frank? What about the women you've been dreaming about here in prison? Are you important to them?

I . . . I . . .

I realized I was just like Johnny. Only I wasn't hung up yet.

And I knew I had to begin looking at my relationships with other people.

7

That night when ten o'clock came and the cells were locked, I was stretched out on my bunk, wide awake, rummaging around in my mind for a place to start. I realized again that here in prison I had nothing. That rarely happens in a guy's life, to have just nothing. No real sense of pride, of accomplishment, of worth, no relationships that are alive enough to be capable of growth and development.

I had Bunny, sure. She came to see me when she could. She had told me when I first came in that she would wait for me if I would promise her I'd go straight when I got out. I knew no dame was going to wait while any guy had to serve out a 22½ year sentence, so I told her to get lost . . . but she still came to see me. I liked that but I knew there wasn't any living relationship there.

How could I have a "living" relationship? Prison reduces men to numbers and file folders and removes any sense of identity. To them, I was really only what my prison jacket said I was.

In another lightning-flicker of self-perception, I realized that I could evaluate everything about myself this way in a truer perspective than I would ever have been able to before. I looked back over the years and saw my life more clearly than I ever had, as if I were another guy standing there looking at it and I knew it was because I had no relationships to cloud my look *at* my relationships.

Just the same, I sure would like to get a look into the stuff the State had crammed into my jacket. Official after official would sit, when he was talking to me, holding the folder open toward his chest so I couldn't see what he was looking at, and drop a hint here and a fact there so that I just bet, what with all of the pre-sentence investigation stuff, he knew everything I'd ever done.

Of course, there wasn't any way he could but that was the impression he tried to give me. The trouble was, you didn't know who they'd talked to, what kind of nuts they'd interviewed about you or what some looney had laid on you that they were now taking as fact about you. I'm sure they saw me in a way I'd never be able to see me.

Loneliness overwhelmed me as I looked back into the years, a loneliness that I somehow recognized was sharpening my perception of myself, my ability to review my relationships with others. That very loneliness was driving me to put into perspective the things in my life which had meaning and the things that did not have meaning.

I had sort of shut the door on relationships that day when I was still in grammar school, and my Dad, eaten up by rejection, had told me my mother was dead. I can still see that satisfied smirk on Tipsy-Topsy's face when he said it.

Since I couldn't remember her anyway, that day really marked the end of any "mother" thoughts for me, but she still had a surprise for me when I went into the Navy.

When I finally got out of that beer hall of a house

in Miami and joined the Navy, I was so happy I was just about drunk myself over the fact that I didn't have to go back to that house anymore. No more fights with Dad, no more haggling with Tipsy-Topsy.

After boot camp, I was assigned to commissary school in Newport, Rhode Island. One weekend I decided to go up to Everett, outside of Boston, to visit one of my aunts. There was this sailor on the base who lived in Everett and we were talking about Everett one night and he said he was going to go up there and that he would take me and pick me up and bring me back if I'd pay him $5 to split the gas bill.

Well, we had visited up there and I had this one aunt who used to come down to Miami and stay with us sometimes and I got along pretty good with her. So I decided to go and visit her and I told the guy I'd go and gave him five bucks.

I had some other aunts on my father's side, too. Actually my father's family was the only family I knew anything about. Anyway, I went with this guy and I got to my aunt's house and she seemed glad to see me and that made me glad I'd gone up there.

We went from her house to some of my other aunts' houses and it was fun, like what a family ought to be. I got to see some of my cousins whom I'd met and known a little during the other trips to Everett and it was a good time. I was glad I went.

It was a good weekend and I felt good that I had gone. On the way back I told the guy with the car I'd like to do it again when he was coming back up there.

A couple of days later I got a call from the Chaplain's office to come and see him. The Chaplain? I couldn't figure what he wanted with me.

I sure hadn't been around him any and I couldn't figure why he'd want me around him.

There were some other guys standing around when I got the message and one of them came up and asked me if I'd like him to go with me.

"Why the hell should I want you to go with me?" He had put his hand on my shoulder and I shrugged it off.

"Well," he said in a nervous kind of way, "sometimes when you get a call to go see the Chaplain like this, it means somebody in your family has died and I just thought you might like to have somebody with you if that's what it was."

I figured the guy was either a creep or a queer and I said, "No, thanks, I can handle whatever he's got for me by myself."

"Okay," he said and walked away and I went to find the Chaplain.

I realized now that as I was walking away from the guy I thought better about him and said to myself I'd look him up when I got back from the Chaplain's office and tell him I appreciated him being concerned . . . but I never did it.

When I finally got there and reported in to the Chaplain, he took me into another office and asked me to sit down. He talked a little bit about the Navy and things and seemed to be a nice enough kind of guy. I kept waiting for all of that God stuff to start but it didn't.

After a while, he said to me, "Frank, you remember when you came into the Navy you were asked to fill out a personnel form?" He had fished a long form out of a stack on his desk and I saw my name on the top of it.

"Yes, sir," I answered.

"Here where it says to list your father's name you've done so," he went on, "but where it asks for your mother's name, you've put deceased . . ."

"Well, I thought with her being dead you didn't need her name, so I just put deceased."

He went right on just as if I hadn't said a word, ". . . and here where it asks for brothers and sisters you've just put down one brother, Robert, who's three years younger than you. Is that right?"

"That's right, sir," I said. I couldn't figure what he was getting at.

Picking up another piece of paper from the pile, he pushed back his chair, rose, and came around and sat on the front edge of the desk about two feet away from me.

"Frank," he said, and his voice was a kind of funny mixture of warmth and confusion, "Why did you put down that your mother was dead?"

Then without pausing for me to answer, he went right on to ask, "and why didn't you list your sister?"

I felt like I was in one of those dreams where everything is going bad and you've got all the handles in your hand to keep them from going bad but no matter what you do everything just keeps on going bad.

"Chaplain," I said and I stood up and I could feel the edge in my voice, "I put down she was dead because she's dead. Dead so long I don't even remember her. Okay?" I started to tell him what he could do with Tipsy-Topsy because I figured she had to be behind all of this but for some reason I didn't. I just went on, "And I didn't put down any sister because I haven't got one. Now would you please tell me what this is all about?"

"What all of this is about is that some girl called

me up trying to find out how to get in touch with you," and he stood up so he was looking at me at eye level, "and she says she is your sister. Does the name Conchetta Costantino mean anything to you?"

"The Conchetta part doesn't," I answered, but in the back of my mind I remembered the old man saying his mother's name was Conchetta.

"I have to confess to you, Frank, that I thought you had put her up to it. She called and gave me this long story about how you all were separated when she was just a kid and she'd never heard of you since until last weekend. She wanted to know if I could get you an emergency pass so she and her mother could see you."

I was totally confused but I knew enough to say, "Well, I didn't have anything to do with it."

"I know that now, Frank," he said, "but then I didn't know whether she was your girlfriend or what, so I told her I would have to look up your records and call her back. I did and all I found was this, so I called her back and said the only Frank Costantino we had at Newport didn't have a sister."

"Well, she wasn't very happy about that and she said she certainly was your sister and you had been up to Everett last weekend to visit your father's family and one of them told her about it and that they knew you were stationed here."

"Were you in Everett last weekend?"

I sank back into my chair. "I don't know what is going on," I said, "but I never heard anything about any sister and my mother's been dead since I was in grade school and I don't even remember her because she left us when I was four or five."

"Did you go to Everett last weekend?"

"Yes, sir. I went to Everett but not to see any

sister. Chaplain, I wasn't even out with any girl at all in Everett." I couldn't figure out what was happening. The feeling of having lost control of what was happening grew, grew along my spine.

"Frank," he said, returning to his chair and picking up another piece of paper, "I think you're going to find she is telling the truth. I think your mother is alive and you have a sister and they both live in Boston and they both want to see you."

"Man," I said, forgetting all about Navy rules, "you're out of your mind."

I started to rise but then I just kind of sank back in the chair as I remembered that day when I was still in grammar school and was so hurt and so mad and I heard myself telling my Dad I was going back to my mother and I heard him saying I couldn't do that because she was dead. I knew now, in some strange way I didn't understand, in this Chaplain's office in Rhode Island that he had been lying. That, tired of having to cope with her memory, he had just said she was dead and so killed her off for all of us from then on.

I looked at the Chaplain and I just said, "I think you're right, Chaplain." I could tell he knew something had happened inside of me.

I just couldn't believe it but I had to. It not only didn't make much sense to me but I didn't really get excited about it. What my father had to say about my mother didn't make me exactly happy over the prospect of meeting her anyway.

The Chaplain went on, "I've fixed up a ninety-six hour pass for you. You can take off right after chow and be in Boston with them for dinner tonight." He was beaming as if he had just put Humpty-Dumpty back together again. Me, I wasn't so sure.

All I could say was, "Thanks, Chaplain," take my pass and get out of there.

Well, I went and when I got off at South Station I met my sister I didn't even know I had and I met my mother, as far as I was concerned for the first time because I really didn't have any memory of her.

It seems that my sister had come out to Everett that day I was there, only I had already been picked up and we were on the way back to Newport. She was talking to one of my cousins and this cousin told her all about me having been there and then told her where I was stationed and that was that.

The reunion wasn't all that great. My mother spent all of the time trying to tell me how hard she had tried to find me and my brother after she had left and how hard my father was to live with and how none of it was her fault but how she always knew her sons would come back and find her.

Well, that wasn't the way it was. I hadn't even tried to look her up because I thought she was dead and from what I had heard about her I wouldn't have tried if I'd known she was alive. I wanted to say, "Hey, lady, that is not the way it is. I haven't come back and found you, I haven't even been looking for you. I didn't even know you existed," but I couldn't do it.

I felt trapped. Trapped in a relationship I wasn't even sure I wanted to be in. I liked my sister all right and I stayed for the rest of my leave but I knew deep inside of me I wanted out.

Some good came out of it though. My brother Bobby came up and stayed with them and that got him away from that bunch of guys he was running with in Miami.

Looking back now, as I lay in my prison bunk, I

knew there had never been a relationship there that was really alive because I didn't want to get into a position where I might be "responsible" for them.

But you took what you wanted from them, Frank.

They offered it.

You always take what you want, Frank.

. . . and there I was trying to go to sleep and that voice, that insistent voice was still talking in my head.

8

As the days rolled by and I kept searching, a kind of detachment came over me and I found myself looking at other incidents in my life, other relationships in my past life as if that life was over, as if I was suddenly in possession of all of the facts of the life of someone else, someone who was dead, like Johnny Wop.

I guess it was because, for me, life had stopped. It was like I had been put in a glass jar and set down in the middle of life. It was going on all around me but I wasn't in it.

I was yesterday's man. I was as removed from the life around me as if I was in an armored car driving right through the middle of life.

Armored cars intrigued me. They could be taken, if you were careful and took your time. I don't mean they weren't dangerous. Any job is dangerous if you're not careful and you could always get blown away by something you didn't have any control at all over, like some drunk running into you or lightning hitting or something like that.

One time Brian Perez, my brother Robert, Arty Hamilton and I were going to rob an armored car. We had been working on this thing for three or four weeks.

The first night I thought about it, I saw the car

coming into the Miami Jai Alai Fronton. I wondered where it had come from and how much it had in it. The next night I went up the road from where it had come about a mile and waited. In a few minutes here it came. For about a week, I tracked it backwards, moving up a dozen or so blocks each night until I had its pattern down.

Since I was sitting in a car waiting, always facing towards them, I didn't have any problem with them making me out. I'd always see them two or three blocks up the road, start the car, come out and take the first turn to the right and be out of sight before they'd ever notice me.

Once, they came out of a side street right in front of me. I started up as soon as they were out of sight, turned into the street they had come out of and then tried to figure out where they'd come from down there. It took me two nights to find out where they were coming from on that street.

It was going to take four of us, so I got Brian, Arty and my brother Bobby, talking to them in that order, one at a time. All three of them wanted in on it.

The next week, I had Brian in a car just a block away from their first pick-up. He followed them to their second pick-up where Arty was waiting to take over. Bobby was waiting at the third pick-up. Then Brian would pick them up again on the fourth and so on. I was at the Jai Alai Fronton.

We began timing the truck. During that week we rotated positions. One time I'd be first, then Robert, then Arty, then Brian. The next night we'd switch around completely, maybe skip one segment. You don't just get on an armored car and tail it all over town.

The next week we followed it out in the other direction. It made two more stops. One at the Pepsi Cola Company where it picked up their receipts for the day and then its final stop was the 27th Avenue Drive-In Theatre toward the end of the second movie.

So naturally, this is the place to grab them. Dark, off the main highway. Pretty deserted. The next night I went to the drive-in movie. I got the schedule. We spent the next week going to the movies. Saturday night seemed the best time. They'd have the biggest haul because of the Fronton.

The driver always brought the guard a cold drink in a cup. The door was open . . . this was the point the score had to focus on. Striking quick while the door was open and getting the thing under control. One bold fast move and it was ours.

On Sunday night the four of us met again. We decided to take it down the next Saturday night. I gave them some other things to do like getting the hot cars. We wouldn't do any tailing at all this week, except for me. I'd tail alone on Wednesday, just to be sure there weren't any changes. I'd skip-tail. Follow a bit, move ahead, wait, follow a bit. Everything was okay, we were on.

Wednesday night, I tailed them some. Everything okay. Thursday, my phone rings. It's a policeman, Charlie Phillips.

He didn't tell me who he was, he didn't have to, he just said, "Meet me at Howard Johnson's."

"Why?"

"I got something to talk to you about," he said. "It's worth a thousand."

I say, "If it's worth a thousand, I'll pay for it."

He asks, "Half an hour?"

"Yeah," I say and hang up.

So I start getting ready to go to Howard Johnson's. Charlie is a real jerk. He's not his own man. In my book, a cop on the take is about the phoniest guy there is. Let them get a chance to blow off in front of some fancy reporter and you'd never hear such high-minded guys . . . and the way they'd talk about us, especially the big shots at budget time, you'd think it was us who was the scum of the earth.

I mean the guys I stole from could always afford it. I didn't steal from no poor people.

In a way I saw myself as a kind of Robin Hood, I guess. Of course, I didn't go giving what I stole to the poor but I was like him as far as stealing from the rich. Even then, they didn't have to pay for what I stole, some insurance company made it up to them.

But cops! You'd see these cops going to church on Sunday and coming around for their pay-off on Monday. Hypocrites! I didn't know how they slept at night. I didn't have trouble sleeping. I didn't do things the guys who were my friends didn't do.

You did not rat somebody out. Okay, I didn't rat anybody out.

You did not talk to policemen when you had a problem with someone. Okay, I didn't talk to policemen when I had a problem.

You did not mess around with the wives of your friends. Okay, I did not mess around with the wives of my friends.

You didn't ever cheat on a partner. Okay, I didn't ever cheat on a partner.

Okay?

If I was in a television show, they might put a black hat on me but they sure as hell wouldn't have me wearing two different hats.

I wouldn't be wearing any gray hat either.

Now here I was having to go and sit down with Charlie and drink coffee with him. He thinks he's slick. Dumb ass. Well, every cop's got a price. There's more policemen ready to take a bribe than there are guys ready to bribe them or able or with the money or the nerve to corrupt them, that's for sure.

I went to Howard Johnson's and I sat down next to Charlie at the counter. We say hello and I order a cup of coffee. I've got a grand in an envelope in my pocket.

Charlie's talking about sports news like I didn't read the morning paper, then he kind of turns toward me and holds his hand out and says, "If you rob the armored truck at the 27th Avenue Drive-In this week-end you're gonna be killed because the cops are going to have the whole place surrounded."

I couldn't figure it. How'd they find out? I just looked at him. He must of thought I wasn't hearing him, because he added, "They're waiting for you every night but they figure you're gonna do it Friday or Saturday 'cause the take'll be bigger."

I wondered who talked. Brian? No, it couldn't be Brian. Bobby? No way. Arty? Hunh unh. I took the envelope out of my pocket and laid it beside his open hand.

"Who?" I asked, looking him dead in the eyes.

He didn't flinch as he answered, "I don't know."

"You can find out," I said. "Find out."

"Okay," he said, "I can find out but it's gonna cost you more."

"So what's new," I said

He's gotta ask questions now, of course it's going to cost more. He needs to ask who the informer is, somebody might ask why he has to know. It's worth more.

I go home working over the names again. Brian? Nawh. Arty? Couldn't be. Bobby. No, he's my brother. Arty? Brian? Round and round. I wondered if the phone could have been bugged. I just had that checked. Some eavesdropping device, maybe? I worried it round and round

The next morning the phone rings, it's Charlie.

"No informer."

"No informer?"

He came back real quiet-like, "No informer." He paused. Then he said, "Meet me at the same place in a half hour."

A half hour later we met. He said hello and ordered coffee. He paused . . . the dramatic pause. The jerk!

Then he began, "A guy by the name of Robert, don't know his last name, was drinking in a bar room, got sudsed up, invited a friend of his to go on the score and the friend was a policeman. He reported it and the set-up is on." He knew my brother's name was Robert but he also knew not to hang that jacket on my brother. I told him I'd get in touch with him later in the day.

Robert! I headed for Bobby's place. When I got there, he was not there but Arty and Brian are waiting for me when I come out and want to know what's up. So I told them.

Now they are some kind of mad, really ready to kill and it's a bad scene. Of course, Bobby's my brother and I'm going to stand up with him. I get them calmed down and they see we don't really know nothing but what a gray hat cop has told me and I leave them to go find Bobby.

When I find him, he's in a bar drinking a beer with a girl. I tell the girl to get lost. She takes one look at me and decides to leave. Bobby gets up and turns on me and sees I'm hot, real hot and he knows whatever it is, it ain't good.

"Sit back down," I say and then I tell him and when I'm through, I say, "What'd you do, get tanked up?"

He says, "No and I don't know what you're talking about."

"You're just like your old man," I said.

He's getting up like he's ready to fight and we have a big, violent argument. He keeps saying he doesn't know what I'm talking about and yet I know he's the only Robert that knows about our plans.

It's now Friday, see, and we're supposed to take that car down Saturday night.

Well, he don't admit that he did this thing. But yet I know that the cops know. I know how they said they got their information. Now we got big problems with Arty and Brian. I tell him to go home and stay there until I call him.

I couldn't figure it. He had me convinced it wasn't him. It sure wasn't like him. He had a temper and he was impetuous but he wasn't a talker, never had been.

So what's with Charlie? What's his angle? And he's got my grand. If Charlie can't tell me more, he's going to have an accident. It's going to be some accident, too.

The trouble is, Charlie would know that. He wouldn't risk having what he knows would happen to him for trying to chump me off. Not for a lousy grand.

I spent the rest of the day and Saturday trying to

find him. No Charlie anywhere.

The next morning the phone woke me up. It was Bobby. He had stayed home the night before, so he had gone to bed early and was up with the birds. He was also very excited.

"Seen the paper?"

"I haven't seen anything," I grumbled. He knew he'd waked me up.

"Well, would you believe," he said, with a smile in his voice I couldn't understand because he knew we had trouble. "Would you believe there's a story here that says three guys got blown away trying to pull down the armored car at the 27th Avenue Drive-In last night?"

It was like a nightmare. I knew I hadn't been out there, I knew Robert couldn't have because he was talking to me on the phone. We couldn't figure it out.

The names of the guys weren't released yet, so we didn't even know if we knew them.

I told Bobby to call Arty and I'd call Brian and let's meet at the bar. I called Charlie at his house and woke him up. "What's the matter?" he asked. I told him about the article. "What?" he said. I told him I needed to see him, and where to meet me.

We had been in the bar about 30 minutes when Charlie came in. He'd been busy checking things out after I'd called him.

We were in a corner booth in an empty bar so it was pretty safe for him.

"Well, that was a pretty good tip, hunh?" he laughed. "Bet you feel a lot better this morning than you'd of felt if you hadn't got it, hunh?" He was not only a gray hat, he was a clown.

I just looked at him, "Tell me about it, Charlie."

"Well," he began, "one of those guys was Robert Walker. He was a cop once but got busted. His mouth. He never learned. He really got busted this time. They were half the night trying to find all of his pieces.

"The cop he invited on the score ratted him out. He goes to Metro and says, 'The armored car is going to be taken down.' He tells them it's going to be done by this guy Robert and a couple of other guys but he don't know who. So they put a helicopter tail on the truck Wednesday night and who do they pick up?"

Twenty pounds of lead suddenly appeared in my stomach. "Me," I said. "In my own car."

Charlie was grinning from ear to ear. "Boy, now things were really buzzing down at Metro. We got big fish in the tank. Frank Costantino! Old Frank who nobody could ever hang one on. Well, you know they figured they just wouldn't even try with this one, it'd just be an ambush and they'd blow you away."

The whole thing had been a coincidence. Both of us working on the same thing at the same time and we were going to take it the same way, almost the same way, at the same location because that really was the best place to take the truck.

Charlie was in high form. "They had the woods full of cops," he said. "Must have been forty or fifty of them. Those guys didn't stand a chance. The minute the first piece showed, they'd had it."

I paid Charlie the "more" I owed him. I still didn't like him but crooked cops come in handy sometimes.

A shiver ran up my spine and some guy in the next cell coughed. I had almost gotten blown away on that job and I began to wonder about it. A nagging sense of fear began to tip-toe around the edges of my mind. It wasn't anything I could identify, it wasn't physical fear or at least no more than a guy usually has in a situation like being in prison where any event can break into violence. I went to sleep trying to pinpoint it.

Frank in the Navy, Cannes, France, 1967.

Frank and Bunny in a popular Miami Beach supper club, 1963.

Left: Frank's wrestling career was a "kick". His primary source of income was stealing.
Below: Wrestling made it possible for Frank to explain large sums of money and his expensive lifestyle.

Frank's wrestling career was short and unspectacular.

Florida State Prison, 1973: Back row—Jerry Spicer, Pete Christian, Bishop William Folwell, Dan Boyer, Frank, Dom Bretti, Bob Erler. Front row—Dennis Bernovich, Jack Murphy.

Jack "Murf the Surf" Murphy, "Nick the Greek" Pirovolas, Joe Donato, Frank "the Godfather", and "Happy Jack" Burbridge in Orlando, 1986.

Above: Frank's ordination, 1979.

Right: Ben Kinchlow from The 700 Club with Frank at Sumter Correctional Institution, 1984.

Below: John Blasi, Frank and Marlin Johnson at Zephyrhills Correctional Institution, 1985.

CBN-TV President Pat Robertson and Frank during filming of Maximum Security.

Frank on PTL with Jim Bakker and Henry Harrison.

Chaplain Ray, Frank and Leola at CPM office in Orlando.

Above: Don Brown and Ted Poitras at site of Christian Prison Ministry Church. Left: Frank and Max Jones.

Nils Schweizer, on behalf of Orlando Mayor Bill Fredrick, presents Frank with a proclamation naming October 26, 1985, "Frank Costantino Day" in Orlando.

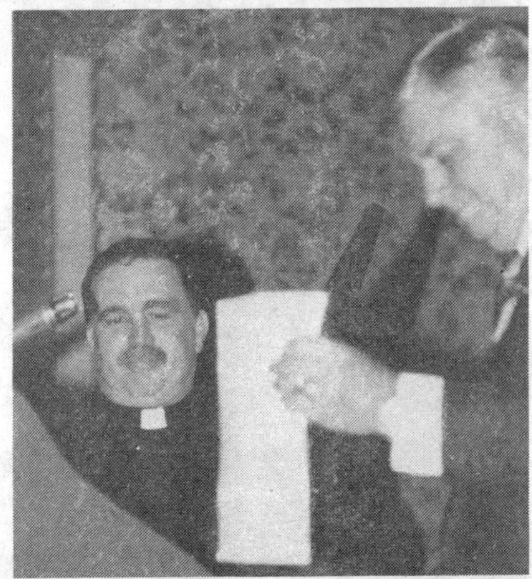

Above: National Prison Invasion planning session. (l-r) Paul Kramer, Larry Kennedy, Paul Carlin, Jim Russo.
Right: Louie Wainwright, Secretary of Department of Corrections, presents Frank with an award for The Bridge from the governor of Florida.

CPM Banquet: Annabel Mitchell, Chairman of Florida Parole Board; Louie Wainwright, Secretary for Department of Corrections; Ellen Morphonious, Circuit Judge from Dade County; Jack Sandstrom, Dade County Department of Corrections; Peggy Sandstrom.

Above: Bunny's dream house.

Left: Bunny as a bride.

Frank and Bunny in front of his grandfather's house, Nichol, Italy.

Frank and Bunny in Naples, Italy, with Kay Poitras.

9

I woke up the next morning still trying to pinpoint it. It had something to do with that armored car action. Something to do with the fact that I was supposed to get blown away in that mess but I didn't. I thought, who says I was "supposed" to get blown away? I didn't get blown away because I was cool, because I was in control.

If I hadn't established contacts with guys like Charlie we might have gotten blown away. The cops had a network of rats who told them what they needed to know. It just seemed natural for us to develop the same network of informers with them. So I had.

Hadn't I done pretty well outside? Forty, fifty robberies a year, that's pretty good. Not only that, but I was getting better all the time. I was using more equipment on my scores, police radios, walkie-talkies, listening devices. We were even looking into the possibilities of using laser beams on future scores.

It's being cooped up like this, being penned in that's causing me to start thinking like this, to wonder what's wrong with me, I thought. There's nothing wrong with me except I got caught. Got caught and didn't have enough clout where it counted at the right time to stay out of here.

I was taking some college couses then I had to write a paper for English 101. The professor said to write what we knew about. Here is what I wrote:

20932

Frank Costantino

Like Colt 45 malt liquor, prison is a completely unique experience. This, of course, is an understatement. Perhaps it was expressed more aptly by a fellow inmate who was evaluating some of his new neighbors. He said, "Here lives the armpit of society."

He was right if he meant that here, within these walls, live the combined rejects of society. These combined rejects make up a society of its own, apart from the world. A sub-normal world, tougher and stricter than any you know, a world without freedom because the people that live here have given up the privilege of responsibility.

The people who are not responsible to a free society because they are not responsible to themselves as individuals give up the privilege of responsibility, the right to be free, and enter a fifth dimension.

Here, life is but isn't, tomorrows are, but mean no more than a day to follow the preceding day. Life is something we can see but not participate in, an intangible reality, truly a fifth dimension. Like shadowy figures, we are but aren't, members of a world which is other than the world we were born to.

Placed here to look out at people who don't realize the importance of what they have, we see the images of ourselves wasting those things which we now see the importance of.

What are the things that are important? To each of us, because we are individuals, this answer varies.

Basically, I believe we all want the same things. The males want to be strong while the females want their males to be strong.

Yet worse than a lack of strength is misguided strength. It's like playing a game of football in which you get knocked around enough so that it's easy to lose sight of the goal but you finally see it and break through six or seven tackles and score a touchdown, only to find out you scored for the other team.

Directing yourself toward the right goal is just as important in the game of life. So, while strength is important to a man and his woman, is it of any use when you score for the other team?

If a man wants to be strong, he wants to be responsible. One is the same as the other. Throw away the right to be responsible and you throw away your right to be strong as a man. Without strength you can not be a man!

"Men who have given up the privilege of responsibility, the fifth dimensional people, are victims of misguided strength. They failed to realize those things which are the most important."

The paper went on to talk about who was important to who and who was responsible to what. What it boiled down to, I said, was that each of us is responsible for our own behavior. Then I ended it with this quotation: "I am the Captain of my ship, the master of my FATE."

It was my own confession of life's darkness. I didn't see . . . man, what a weak defense that is. I didn't see. I wondered how many other people might feel this way or even how many really ever "saw" like I was seeing right then . . . past emotional involvement into some segment of truth. Truth about myself.

I had to shake these thoughts. Too much of this kind of thinking could drive me out of my gourd.

Deep inside I knew I was who I was and good or bad, there was no undoing what was done. All I could do was go on from where I was. Build a new life on who I was, from where I am.

Well, maybe I was blind to a lot of things but in many ways I was better than these creeps around me, and when it is all said and done I'll do what I have to do.

That night in my bunk that voice was at me again. *You may be the Captain of your ship, Frank, but look what happened to the people who had to share this world with you.*

I never hurt anybody who wasn't trying to hurt me. I just did what I had to do.

How about that guy at the phone booth, Frank? How about him?

The guy at the phone booth? That creep? Butting into something that wasn't any of his business. Well, he got his!

Yeah, Frank. He got his because you're a taker, you take what you want, Frank.

I thought about those days in the early sixties. There was good money in phone booths. It was very lucrative way of making a living for a young guy. A pay telephone had like $150 in it when it was full.

A good team, two guys, could crack open 10 or 15 of them in a night very easily at that time. That was a lot of money in 1961. I was 22 years old and that was $700 to $1,000 each, every night we worked. Like a month's pay to most guys and no taxes.

I thought I had arrived. I had a guy by the name of Fat Dog working with me and we did the eastern seaboard from Florida to Maine and back.

We'd move into a town, get a motel room, then case the next town up or down the road, mapping out the most likely booths during the day. Then that night we'd hit them and be on our way. We went in a zig-zag pattern so they never knew where we were going to hit next, even if they were tracking where we'd hit, which I don't believe they ever did.

We had worked our way up the coast and all the way back to Miami by the time this creep showed up. It was a screwy evening anyway. I was prying open the first booth we hit that night when the phone rang as I was bending the tire iron back. It was an eerie sound, like it was alive and hurting. I stuck the tire iron way up inside it and jabbed and twisted it until the ringing stopped.

Maybe there was a message there after all. Maybe it was a call for me.

A half an hour later and a mile away, we'd just done this phone booth and were taking off and this guy comes beeping up behind us and begins trying to pull us over. Adrenaline shot through my system, pumping, pumping.

We had maybe $15,000 in coins in the car and a trail of busted-open pay phones behind us and here is this off-duty cop beeping up out of nowhere.

Think! Think! My first impulse was to take off but that was useless. If he didn't have a radio, he could find a phone booth within two blocks and we'd be nailed within minutes. I decided to play it cool. I didn't think he had seen us busting that box open. I think he just came up right after us, saw the box split open and took off after us. I told Fat Dog to stop.

The adrenaline was slowing down. I was getting cool. Be cool, I thought. He was almost right beside us now, trying to force us over to the curb. Dog looked around, gave him that surprised, "Who, me?" look and pulled over.

He pulled right in behind us, dimmed his lights and got out. He crossed between the cars and came up on my side and I got out. Fat Dog got out, went to the back of the car, crossed between them and came up behind him. The guy was yelling at me as he came.

He had nerve, I'll give him that. I guess he was tough, wherever he came from. Anyway, he was calling us punks and telling me to do this and do that and all of a sudden he was talking about making a citizen's arrest.

Wow! He wasn't a cop at all, no plainclothesman, no nothing. Just a hero. I let the tire iron I had up my sleeve slip down into my palm as I stepped toward him and Fat Dog grabbed him from behind.

I poked him straight in the gut with it. If it had been a knife, it would have gone clean through him. He let out this "whooooofff" of air and grabbed at his stomach and as he did I caught him with the flatside of the iron against the side of his face.

Then I began to really work him over with it. And he grunted and began to cry and he wasn't so tough any more . . . and I got more and more cool and I just worked him slowly, from side to side, up and down his body.

It was a truck tire tool and there was some weight to it and I used the weight so it sunk into him. He was slobbering now and crying and begging and I just kept working him over. He'd never ever make any other citizen's arrest. I just keep hitting him and I was wondering why I was doing this. It was as if I was standing outside of myself and watching somebody else doing it. There was an unrealness about it.

Suddenly, he went limp on us and Fat Dog dropped him. He was very badly beaten and the blood was oozing out of his mouth and nose. I told Fat Dog to get in the car, go up the street and turn around and come back down and I'd shove this hero, this citizen's arrest hero, out in front of the car and we'd make it look like a hit-and-run.

So he did. He went up to the next block and turned around and was coming back down toward us when another car turned into the street from the opposite direction. It was now very early in the morning, three o'clock, maybe. Adrenaline again.

I just dropped the guy on the side of the road and started running toward the car as Fat Dog slowed down. I whipped the door open, jumped in and we were off.

The guy had to be dead anyway. The guy in the other car stopped to look at him, then spun to follow us. We lost him before he turned the first corner. I was cool again. We started home.

We didn't get to stay there long. The guy wasn't dead. He was still conscious, he had our tag number and car description written down in his car and he told the guy in the other car who had gone right back to him when he lost us.

He had the police on the phone in two minutes and gave them a description of us too. We had dumped the loot and had just walked in the door of my pad when they arrived.

Big stuff! I was bonded out right away. This "hero" was some kind of mad. He was out for vengeance. When the case came up I waived a jury trial and we went to court before Judge Ben Willard.

We were up on two misdemeanor counts on one set of charges: entering without breaking a structure and damaging telephone equipment. I got sentenced for damaging telephone equipment but the sentence was suspended and I was acquitted on the entering without breaking charge.

So much for that.

But, we were up for assault with intent to commit murder against the hero at the same time. It had been more than six months since that night when we got into court so he didn't show any signs of the massive beating he'd gotten. In an attempt to make up for the disappeared bruises, he fell into the temptation to overstate what had, in fact, happened to him.

He was telling the judge that we beat him with a sledge hammer or a crow bar and that he heard me say let's throw him out in front of the car and run over him and the judge just didn't believe him.

And actually it had happened . . . most of what he was saying . . . it was so incredible that he didn't have to add much to it because it was a very brutal beating but he even added to that, which people tend to do. I think it is just very normal, natural, when you tell a story about something that has happened, a traumatic story, that you add to it. I don't think it's possible to tell it the way it really happened.

Anyway, this guy didn't. Our hero was now under the spotlight or in it and he started talking about all of the blood and reeling a bit and he said something about being hit with a sledge hammer and he began to lose the judge.

"You mean to tell me," the judge said, "that two men weighing more than 200 pounds apiece beat you for fifteen minutes with a sledge hammer or a crowbar or whatever it was and you weren't unconscious and heard them plotting to run over you with their car?"

He didn't believe it. We were charged with just assault and convicted and given a fine of $100 or 30 days in the county jail. I paid the fine and we still had $1,300 left from that night's work. Well, we had some lawyer's fees to pay and a bondsman's fee. It could keep you broke if you didn't keep working.

I kept cool, so I kept in control. The Captain of my ship . . . and I dozed off to sleep.

10

I slept fitfully for a few minutes then I knew I was awake again because I was tense all over, just like I was waiting for somebody to hit me or something. That fear, that unknown fear was back, driving sleep out of my body, out of the cell.

Then that voice: *If you're the master of your fate, what are you afraid for?*

And I didn't know. I wasn't physically afraid. I thought about it over and over. I had the rest of the day off and I just laid there in my bunk and thought about it.

Why am I afraid? What am I afraid of? I'm resenting something. What am I resenting? Imprisonment? Sure, I resent that. Anyone would. The control over me? That's it! I'm being pushed around all the time, every week I get pushed around. What are they liable to try next week?

I tried to understand the guards, the people who had this direct contol over my life without my own emotional involvement.

Maybe they didn't like the life they were leading anymore than I liked mine. The head of the prison system, a guy by the name of Louie Wainwright, was quoted in a newspaper as saying zoo keepers get paid more than prison guards. How is that for a grabber? Well, maybe zoo keepers had to know more. These guys didn't even have to know how to read or write, let alone have a high school education.

Maybe they were angry too, angry about the takers who had things they didn't have. Angry about their lives or jobs or homes.

I began again to be able to see myself a little bit as if I was in someone else's shoes, to see how they felt. When that insight began to come, an increasing awareness crept over me of a far greater prison than the concrete and steel I saw around me.

How does it feel, Frank?

How does what feel?

How does it feel to be the pushee, Frank? Like that guy at the phone booth. To be the pushee and not the pusher?

It's frustrating. Not having any control over your own life.

How does it feel to be a nobody on the road to nowhere . . . just like a million other people?

That's why any little victory over the system is so important. When you win one, you hang onto it. It helps to rebuild a sense of identity.

And I turned a corner in my mind and I was walking against a torrent of people on a busy, busy street and as they streamed past me I became aware that I knew all of them and that I was the only guy on the street going in the opposite direction . . . they were all looking at me . . . and right through me.

They didn't stop, they didn't even pause, they just sort of looked at me and dismissed me, the way you'd glance at yesterday's newspaper blowing in the wind. I was trying to speak, but the words wouldn't come. I was trying to stop some of them, to get their attention, to get them to speak to me, but they just gave me that yesterday look and went on by. I felt invisible.

And I was screaming at them,"Hey, stop! It's me, it's Frank, this is Frank Costantino in this skin," but no one heard me.

Why the interest in them Frank? You never really cared for them out there.

Yeah, I did. I liked them. I liked almost all these people.

Just as you "liked" big cars, juicy steaks, alligator shoes, Frank. What about love, Frank?

Well, sure, man. Some of these people loved me. I had money, and I was a well known hood. There was stock in being seen on the street with me. Money made a man respected and I made money.

Hey, Frank, look. There comes one that didn't love you because of what you had or what you could give her. She just loved you because you needed to be loved and she needed to love.

Bull! Everybody that loves somebody loves them because of something they can get out of them.

How about these people, Frank?

And the character of the surging crowd changed. It changed in size to a dribble, to just a few scattered people on the sidewalk and it changed to people who looked at me and smiled and came up and stopped and touched me and asked how I was and what they could do for me.

There was a girl I had known in high school; my football coach, who was really concerned; a girl I'd known in Boston; a teacher I had had in elementary school; and Bunny. She loved me that way and was always saying things like, "All I want is you, not things." An Irish-Catholic bartender I knew who used to talk God to me and told me he prayed for me that when I finally go caught, I wouldn't get killed. Funny, Huh? Well, I hadn't got killed. I guess he thinks somebody answered his prayer.

And all of a sudden I realized I wasn't being looked through anymore. I was in prison blues and still they were coming up to me and talking and showing their love for me.

What did they get out of you, Frank? What did they love you for? What was the "because" with them, Frank?

I don't know. I never had that kind of love for anybody. I never knew you could love somebody like that . . .

You never knew it, Frank? Or did you think it was weakness?

Well, I . . .

You mean you were never willing to risk it, don't you?

Well, I'm not about to let somebody chump me off! You never know how somebody'll screw you if you go letting yourself go, getting emotional over things.

You're just a lot better off if you pay for everything you get, then you don't owe anybody anything . . . you're not in anybody's debt . . . you go start letting somebody know how you feel, and they can use it against you like a lever. Never show the areas you are vulnerable in, that could get you killed.

Nawh. You're a lot better off to play it cool, man. Keep people at a distance. Especially women, women are like a bus, as a guy once said, there's one coming every five minutes.

Brian, he got all mixed up with a broad like that and look what happened to him. He was one of the best guys I ever worked with. He was like a brother to me, and look what happened to him. If he had kept away from Dolores, he'd have been okay. Me, I stayed away from Dolores' pad except on business.

My relationship with Dolores was purely business. She was a fence and a pretty good one, though she'd screw you too if she got a chance. She had a yearning for flashy Cadillacs and good looking men and my work helped her pay for some of both. She was a bad scene and finally cost me some heat.

I had a couple of partners at the time. Arty Hamilton and Brian Perez. Brian was a big, tall, good looking guy. Six-foot-two, dark, wavy black hair, about 26, a real stud. The three of us were stealing and doing pretty good. We used to go into a restaurant, The Red Oven in Hialeah, Dolores and her husband, Paul, owned.

Then Paul and Lennie, it was kind of an odd set-up, both of them were in love with Dolores, but not odd if you knew Dolores . . . anyway, Paul and Lennie got busted on a robbery and Dolores began to give me tips about places. We'd hit the place, and if it was any good, she'd get fifteen percent for the tip. If we didn't get anything worth while, then she didn't get anything.

It was a good deal. She had sources all over the county feeding her information about things. So if she gave you a tip that led to a score which was worth a hundred grand it was better than if you go out and steal something you only get five for, huh? So I was glad to pay the fifteen percent. She had nerve, too. You had to give her that.

She said she really needed money to get a lawyer for Lennie. I guess Paul already had one. Anyway, she gave us five or six really good leads in a row about then.

Brian fell in love with her. He began to spend all of his time over there. Every time we wanted him, we found him with Dolores. Arty came and talked to me about it. He was worried about us getting cut off from her, about her putting Brian out on the street alone. I was worried too, but not so much about that. Dolores was a smart woman and Brian was a romantic kid, no match for her in any way.

I liked Brian and I didn't want to see him get hurt. We could all have trouble if she decided to use him. Her husband, Paul, and Lennie might be in jail, but Brian was not in their league. Dolores was playing lots of other games, too. It made me nervous.

I talked to Brian about it and he just wouldn't hear a word out of me about her.

"You guys just don't understand her," he told me one day. "That's my woman and I love her," he said, and he said it with that kind of finality that ends a converstion and so I said okay, but I hurt for him.

A week or so later he comes up to me and wants to know can I loan him a thousand. I could but I wanted to know for how long. He said Dolores needed it and I could have it back in a week. I told him I was loaning it to him, not to Dolores, and I would expect it back the next week.

Well, the next week went by and the next and the next. Then I went over the the Red Oven one night and I asked him when he was going to pay me my thousand bucks.

"You know, Brian," I said, "You promised to pay it back in one week and it has now been three I don't like that."

"Jeez, Frank," he said, "I know, but just haven't

got it. I haven't been doing anything and I just haven't got it. I haven't had a job in weeks."

That made me mad. He was lying and I knew it. Two weeks before, Mo had brought me a score that he and Brian had stolen and asked me to fence it for him in New York. I had done it and sent Brian his end, which was $9,000. Now, Brian didn't know I was the one that sent it to him but I knew he had gotten it. I did what I had to do.

So I said to him, "I know you have the money, Brian, you and Mo both have money right now." His eyes widened with surprise, but before he could say anything, Dolores jumped into the discussion, saying she knew he didn't have any money.

I cut her off. "No, Dolores," I said, "this isn't any of your business. This isn't you. This is Brian and he has got to pay." She understood that, so she moved down the counter a little way but not so far she couldn't hear what we were saying.

Brian started arguing again and we really got into it. She had her hooks into him good and he was just feeding his money to her. Her appetite for money was insatiable and that was okay with me just as long as it wasn't my money. The fifteen percent was hers and that was all. She earned it but she didn't earn my thousand I loaned to Brian. You start letting that kind of thing slip and pretty soon somebody would be taking you for soft, then taking you for more.

Well, nobody was going to take me for anything. And what the hell was I arguing with Brian for anyway? He owed me the money, didn't he? He'd said he'd pay it back in a week and it was now three wasn't it?

So I said to him, "Okay, Brian, you got a couple of

days. Either meet me and pay me or you and I are going to get serious." And I got up and looked at Dolores and walked out.

She was furious, I could tell it. Her face got all stiff and she gave me a look straight from the pits of hell. A guy I knew called me the next day and said Dolores had gone straight down to the Dade County Jail to see Paul and Lennie and told them I was in there threatening Brian and her.

Lennie had known me for a long time and apparently he tried to calm her down but she really laid a number on him. She was good at that sort of stuff and she hyped both Lennie and Paul to try to get them to put pressure on me from the jail.

The guy quoted her as saying, "Well, you know, I don't know about Frank. He's mad and you know how he is. He might hurt me." I thanked the guy for the news and asked him if Lennie and Paul had sent him to me. That really scared him, that question did. He said no in several ways and left in a hurry and I knew he went straight to Dolores, which was okay by me. Maybe she'd get right enough to give Brian back my money and save his life.

Apparently she did because Brian called me the next day and said he had the money and if I'd meet him at the Boots and Saddle Bar he'd pay me. I met him and he paid me.

Then I told him that as far as I was concerned, my beef with him was over.

"But," I added, "you're not my friend anymore and let's just go our separate ways from here on. You make me nervous with your Dolores. I just don't want to do any more business with you. I don't like the way you handled this."

He began to argue with me but I was through. I

wasn't mad at him, he'd paid me the grand and he was okay with me. I just didn't want to be involved with a guy hypnotized by a broad.

"It's over, man," I said. "When you get rid of Dolores, let me know. I got nothing against you." And I left.

A week later I got a call in my office at Decor Originals, the company I owned. It was a friend of mine.

"I got some bad news for you, Frank," he says.

"Yeah," I answered.

"Your buddy, Brian, got it last night . . . and that ain't all. His girl friend, Dolores Costello, went with him," he said.

"And . . . ?"

"Nothing, I just thought you ought to know. It was an execution, man. Both of them handcuffed with their hands behind them. They were in her pad, in her bed. It's a good thing Paul's in jail."

"Yeah," I said. "What else?"

"Nothing, that's all. Just thought you'd want to know."

"Thanks," I said, "I'll be seeing you around. Let me know if you hear anything." I thought about asking him if they had found anything I ought to know about when they searched her place but nixed the idea. No point in putting any ideas in his head. So I hung up.

Late that evening, I drove by the Red Oven but it was all closed up. I stopped and picked up the paper and read the account. It was big news and ran for days. I went to see Arty and he was hurting real bad over it. So was I, I just didn't say so. Brian was a good friend.

The funeral was a cops and robbers game. Unless

you'd been around awhile, you couldn't tell which side some of the people were on. Paul was there, accompanied by a deputy. So was Lennie. I wondered how he'd pulled that. So was the D.A. He was looking for information.

I didn't know what people might tell him but I thought I had better get myself covered for the time of executions. I had a friend who was a police chief of a little town out in the county and we had an arrangement.

I went to a pay phone and called him. When I got him on the line, I told him to call me and gave him the pay phone number. In about five minutes, the pay phone rang.

"Yeah?" I asked.

And he asked, "Frank?"

"Yeah."

"What's up?"

"I think I might need some cover," I said, "on the Costello murders. I don't know who blew them away but I've got an idea somebody might try to hang this thing on me."

"Sure, Frank," he said. "When and for how long?"

I told him the day and hour I wanted to be booked in and when I wanted to be booked out.

"All fixed," he said. "I'll have you on the blotter inside a half hour."

I told him thanks and said I'd take care of him right away.

"No hurry, Frank, it's my pleasure," he answered and hung up.

Anyway, now if they tried to hang this thing on me, I could prove I had been in jail when it happened. They did try. That afternoon they picked me up and took me downtown for questioning.

Lennie had told them Dolores had come to him and Paul in jail and told them I'd said I was going to blow her and Brian away.

I let them go through the whole thing. All the inuendos, all the traps, all the threats, but they didn't really have a thing on me. I was cool. I had the jail thing in reserve but I never had to use it.

They let me go and I left thinking how I would have to have a talk with Lennie.

So, see what letting people inside does to you? Brian found out. It cost him all he had. She chumped him off, okay, with the big final one. Dolores had her hooks in him.

11

Realizing that my hands were clenched, I knew I had drifted into that restless sleep again, my body rigid on the bunk, waiting for the blow to strike.

Then that vision of those people on that almost empty street who had been reaching out to me returned.

Are these women like that, Frank? Is Bunny like that, Frank? Do new ones like them come along every five minutes?

And I knew they didn't. There weren't any . . . any conditions attached to their love. Like another flash of lightning in the dark recesses of my mind, I suddenly knew I had never loved like that. There were always conditions to my love.

That's why you weren't able to respond to their love, Frank, why it never really meant anything to you.

. . . and I knew that was right. I got out of it just what I put into it. Superficial things. Sex. Comfort. I realized that more had really been given to me than I received, because I wouldn't accept it.

"You thought, with women, it was all just sex, Frank, and you thought you were pretty good at that. But they all just passed you by on that crowded street back there, just looked through you uncaring and passed you by. Why, Frank? Why?

. . . and I knew that most of my relationships with women had been for the sex, for the coupling, and I knew there was more than that. There was a deeper meaning in relationships with women and maybe even sex could be an expression of that deeper meaning . . . something other than just the conquest and the thrill.

Remember that hooker in Boston? Remember how she said, "I'd rather sleep with an ice-cold German than with a red-hot wise guy?"

You really laughed at that, didn't you?

Yeah, yeah, I see it now. A red-hot wise guy is not a guy a woman can have an experience with . . . she could only be a part of his experience . . . with himself.

Why couldn't you share with people, Frank? Why couldn't you share Frank with people?

That wasn't important to me and it appeared as weakness.

What was important, Frank?

To be cool, to be detached. To show strength. To show that nothing scared me, nothing touched me. That I was always the same. Untouchable, by anything, or anybody. The way to be cool was not to be uncool. The way not to be uncool was don't get emotional, keep things under control.

Do you think women are weak?

Women are into emotions. Not just in the bedroom but all the time. The key to life is to keep things under control, that applies to everything. Love, women, emotions, even stick-ups. The key to a good stick-up is control. I remember once—I could almost laugh about it now, but I almost got myself blown away once because I couldn't see what was going on. Literally. A score out of control.

I'd been walking downtown in Hollywood, Florida, one day, where I'd gone to meet a guy about a deal he had working. Out of this department store comes this lady decked out with ice and what looked like at least a 10 carat hoop on her finger. It was the kind of stuff that told you when you saw it that there was plenty more of the same at home.

She pauses at the curb and up comes her chauffeur with his Rolls limousine. I was parked at the corner on the side street and I took off with only two cars between us. I followed her right to the entrance of her estate on the inland waterway in Hollywood, always with one or two cars between us.

It was a big house, though the grounds weren't much in size. The chauffeur wheeled into a circular driveway, stopped and helped her out at the front door. Then he eased the car away and around a side driveway toward the garage on the west side of the house.

It was quite a place. There was a sign, very fancy, on the iron fence along the street which warned you to beware of bad dogs. One side of the property faced the inland waterway, one side faced the street, one side joined a neighbor's property and part of the fourth side was also on the water.

I spent three weeks studying that place, learning what I could of the layout and the operation of the house. By then I knew that the house was elaborately wired with very sophisticated alarm systems and at night, a pair of Dobermans roamed the fenced lawns. The only access to the house which would avoid them was through the front door during the day.

I knew the times the owner, who was a widow, regularly left and returned to the house. I knew the number of servants and what their schedules were. I had also picked the guys I wanted to work with me on the job. I was convinced there was a safe in the house because, though she went out several times while I was watching her really loaded with ice, she never went to a bank but once during that time and then she wasn't getting into any safety-deposit box.

The guys who were going in with me were Brian Perez, Mo Durrall, who was a southern guy, tough but really mellow and Bill Hart, a guy built like a wrestler who wasn't right bright but was dependable and Mo really liked him.

Every single detail of the entry was planned. We had a hot van. The plan called for us to drive up to the front door of the house, one of us to get out and go up to the door with a bouquet of flowers, come down on whoever opened the door and lead the way for the next two who would follow in right behind him. Once inside, everybody knew exactly what they were supposed to do and how we planned to restrain the servants.

It was planned down to the last minute detail. There wasn't anything wrong with the plan but Bill screwed the whole thing up. I drove the van, Bill and Mo met me near the Hollywood circle where they had parked their cars. Brian was in the van with me. I picked Bill and Mo up and they sat cross-legged on the van floor beside the sliding door on the side of the van which would be facing the house steps. Brian rode shot-gun.

As we drove into the driveway of the house, Mo handed Brian the bouquet and as I stopped next to the steps Brian swung out and up the steps to the door where he rang the bell. He was the only one of us whose face would be seen by anyone. Mo and Bill had stocking masks over their faces and I wore a mask made of one half of a pair of Bunny's light tan knit pants. That's the kind of mask I always wore.

I would whack them off at the knees, cut them in half from the middle of the waist through the crotch, pull it down over my head beginning with the waist end in front and end up with what used to cover her hips covering my chest. The open end would be laid over on top of my head. All I had to do was cut two eye holes. With that tan color and a cap on my head, no one more than twenty feet away would know I was wearing a mask unless they looked me right in the face.

It was all going like clockwork. Everything was cool. I pulled the pants leg down over my head, adjusted it so that the eye holes were in the right place, put my cap on and glanced back up at the doorway. The front door was swinging open and there stood the larger of the two maids. Brian handed her the flowers and pulled his piece.

The score was coming down. I said "go" and as I went out and around the front of the van, I heard the sliding door open as Mo and Bill leaped out. I looked up into the doorway and saw Brian suddenly double over forward and heard his piece smack as it slammed onto the marble floor of the entrance hall.

He let out a pained "Yooouuumph" and staggered sideways as Mo and I started toward him.

I realized the maid had kneed him in the crotch. Bill, who was supposed to swing left and cover the kitchen door, froze, undecided whether to come to Brian's aid or block the exit to the garage and street.

Brian, wild with pain, reached up and grabbed the maid by the hair, yanking her face toward him as he swung toward it with his right fist. I hit the top step as she collapsed into a heap on the floor. Mo, who was one step ahead of me, jumped over the collapsed maid and swung to the right where something had moved.

Brian shouted to me to go to the left as he pointed to a door that was just closing at the left end of the entrance hall. I hit the door on a dead run and was in the butler's pantry where two women cowered against a counter on my left. My momentum carried me right through the pantry to the kitchen where I saw the butler fleeing through the side door, screaming "We is being robbed! We is being robbed!" as he ran through the side lawn and up the street.

Great! The whole score was out of control!

I spun back into the butler's pantry and grabbed the nearest of the two women I had almost run over as I came through. She was very frightened and started to fight. As she pulled back from me, she yelled "Helen" at the top of her voice and the other woman, who was obviously Helen, came at me with an umbrella.

I couldn't believe it. This crazy broad was taking me on with an umbrella. Me. Frank Costantino! I thought about blowing her away but checked myself immediately. "That's crazy, man. Get hold of yourself. She's scared out of her mind."

I raised my arm to block the blow and bent my head at the same time. She had a real Babe Ruth home-run swing and she brought it around barely missing me, but knocking my hat across the room. Out of nowhere suddenly comes a poodle who buries his teeth in the top of my calf. I could feel the teeth sinking in as I tried to shake him loose.

While I'm reaching for the poodle, I hear two

sounds at once. One is the growling of the dog and the other is the sound of shattering glass. It was a moment before I realized the glass had shattered on my head and large pieces of it were splattering onto the floor around me.

The woman I had grabbed had picked up a large glass something-or-other and cracked me over the head with it. I looked at her. Her hands were reaching to cover her open mouth. She was scared, whether of me or over having broken the glass over my head, I didn't know.

Just as I got a grip on the dog's throat, this other dame connected with that umbrella right against the side of my jaw and an instant later I got the mate to the first piece of glass. There was broken glass and blood everywhere and as I turned toward the umbrella-wielding woman, I caught her with one arm, caught the glass breaker under my other arm, and started toward the door with the poodle still hanging onto my left leg.

As I turned, I slipped on the blood which was pouring from my leg onto the tile floor and all four of us went down in a heap. The two women, the dog and me. As we began to fall, one of the women grabbed at my head and pulled my mask around sideways, leaving me in absolute darkness, unable to see anything.

When we hit the floor, the smaller of the two women was underneath me and I heard her breath being knocked out of her as she landed on her back. The sound of her head thudded like a melon as it hit the tile. She really went out.

I grabbed the other broad with both hands and put an arm lock on her . . . too hard and too fast. I'd done that a hundred times as a wrestler but never had tried it on a woman before. I heard the bone break. She screamed once, then fainted.

I was sitting in the middle of the pantry floor as I straightened my mask and reached for the dog who was still clinging tightly to my calf. Blood was everywhere. The poodle's white face and body were covered with blood, the floor was splattered with blood. It looked as if there had been a massacre in there.

"You're dead poodle," I said, grasping his throat with both hands. I squeezed until he went limp, squeezed some more, then pried him loose from my leg.

The score was out of control. With that guy yelling down the street, we had to get out of here, quick.

Just then, Mo came in the pantry, asking "Is everything under control here?"

I told him about the guy who was already out and told him we had to cut out. The broad I had landed on was our pigeon. I hadn't recognized her up close, but now I realized that's who she was. She was still wearing that gob of ice. We took the hoop off her finger and ran for the van.

Fear was growing in my chest as I started the van. The cops were probably on the way. I swung out of the drive and up the street to the boulevard, then right toward the circle. Then I saw the cops coming toward us, no sirens, but really hauling it.

I knew it was a pinch as they bore down on us. We were really had. There wasn't anywhere to turn, nowhere to go. We were just goners. They were a block from us, a half a block and I braced for the spin I knew they were going to make.

They went right by us. They didn't even look at us.

I realized they didn't even know about the van. Not yet. That gave us some time, not much but some. I slowed down a bit. All we needed now was to get stopped for speeding or some stupid mistake.

We got to the circle, I drove us around behind Moyes Chinese Restaurant, we ditched the van and in two minutes were back in our cars headed home. We were lucky just lucky . . . not cool at all.

It wasn't until a week later that I thought about how crazy the whole thing was. Who'd ever expect a maid to knee a guy like Brian? Brian was six-two and weighed one-eighty. He was a lot of man. Well, women who smile and say what they think you want to hear, like Dolores used to do with Brian, were just as tricky as that broad was. They don't trick me, I'll tell you that.

How do you keep from getting tricked by a woman, Frank?

How do I know; I just didn't get involved, uninvolved is not to get your nose open. I've heard more than one guy on the street say that. "Don't get your nose open over a chick," they'd say. "If you get your nose open, she'll lead you around."

My step-mother did that with my father and I have hated her for it ever since. Whenever I would see her characteristics in a woman, I would cut out. No big story. No big thing. Just pack up and go.

I drifted off to sleep again. A restless sleep in which I dreamed of my father with a ring in his nose and this long chain fastened to the ring.

12

That dream disappeared and when I awoke again in that long night, I knew I had crossed some sort of bridge. I couldn't figure out what it was or when in my dream it had happened but I knew I was in a new place with myself.

I searched back through my mind to my conscious thoughts and I thought of all of those people who had offered me love with no strings attached, requiring no submission to their will and I wondered if I wouldn't rather have had a relationship in which I experienced something of that other person instead of always just experiencing Frank Costantino no matter who I was with or what I was doing.

I was tired of just me. I never realized it was an either-or matter like that. I always wanted to be macho, act like a man. Even when I was a kid, I used to watch the cowboy movies and they were always like . . . well, you know, like the Lone Ranger would ride off into the sunset, leaving the girl pining away back at the ranch.

The realization came to me that my inhibitions, my pride, my own macho image kept me from ever expressing my love in return, kept me from being expressive of who I was, of what I was. My macho image had been more important to me than any relationship I was ever in.

That voice in me began to push at me.

What do you think now, Frank?

I don't know. I just don't know . . .

Who has had the richer experience, Frank, you with your macho distance or the people who have loved you, who have fully felt and lived what they felt regardless of the price.

But I never felt like that, I never had that kind of feeling.

Yes, but you wanted to feel it Frank, you wanted to but you were afraid to. Afraid of what you might do. Afraid of what you might say. Afraid of the cost, Frank

Afraid? Me, afraid? No way.

No. Not in any physical sense, Frank, but fear of rejection forced you to control every relationship you ever had so rigidly that you never really participated in it. Your very fear has kept you from trying a real relationship.

Yeah, but . . . and I opened my mind about that. It was true.

My trouble now, I began to see, was that I ran hot and cold about everything I did or thought I wanted to do, about everything I thought about in terms of where I was and where I was going.

I'd taken an extension course in Psychology 101 and had been down that road of B.F. Skinner's and I just didn't buy all of that crap. It sounded good. It was a good excuse for what I had done, but I didn't really think that a laboratory mouse's reactions to things necessarily proved that I reacted the same way for the same reasons.

. . . but one day I would find myself agreeing with

the behaviorists and the next day I would find myself unable to believe any of it. Hot and cold. Hot and cold. Hot and cold.

There would be some days when, for no reason I could see, I would be on top of the world. Then for no reason I could see, I'd be at the bottom of the pit. It didn't seem to have anything to do with my body, with the way I felt physically, so I decided it had to be a mental outlook.

The trouble with that was, when I really analyzed the way I felt and how I got there, it didn't all seem to be a mind-type thing. There was something else, something tied to that voice deep within me, that other me.

In that sort of in-and-out state of sleep just before you doze off, I suddenly realized that I had to make up my mind, once and for all.

I really had to work at suppressing who I was in any relationship, suppressing the fact that I really did want to let myself feel love, that I really did want to give, that I did really want to participate . . . that I actually, to protect my macho image, had to work at suppressing who and what I was so that I might fit the mold of the guy that I thought I ought to be . . .

And what's he like, Frank?

I'm not sure, I've never let him out. I didn't really know all this before, who I am really. I don't even know what I'm like.

What do you want to be like, Frank?

I want to be exactly who I am, to show exactly who I am, nothing more, nothing less. I am not a phoney, I just didn't see what was happening with me.

Do you have the guts to be real?

I have the guts to say something hurts if it hurts.

to say I enjoy something or somebody if that's the way I feel. Even if somebody else thinks the way I feel is corny. I think that's where real courage is. And I have courage.

Is being real more important than being cool?

Yes, being real is more important. I liked the sound of that in my mind and I said it again, mouthing the words in the darkness. "I honestly think being real is more important than being cool." Yeah, because looking back, there're lots of places I don't even know how I felt about something. All I can remember is how I acted when it was said, or when it happened . . . how cool I was in the face of whatever it was.

Not being real is . . . well, it's being unreal, being a fake, being a fraud and that . . . I can't swallow that, man.

I want to know where I've been. I want to know what's happened to me. I want to know who I am.

Have you got the guts to be that honest, Frank?

I've got the guts, I just didn't see this before.

I started reading, all the time. I read all the guys who were supposed to know what went on. I read Plato, read what he said about Socrates, got my mind around his concept of an ideal. I read Aristotle. I couldn't understand a lot of what they were talking about, but I read on and on.

I even tried the Bible but that really left me out in left field. I just got through . . . no I didn't even get through three books, I stopped before I had finished the third book. It was all about don't do this and don't do that and you've got to do this and you've got to do that. Well, it wasn't talking to me. I was looking for the truth.

I wasn't looking for a lot of rules.

I didn't need to be a thief but it didn't bother me to do it.

That Bible book was just like those preachers that used to come into the Dade County Jail and harangue you. I remember this one guy used to come. He was always telling about how God sat up there watching everything we did and he had this big book, see? And every time we did something wrong, something he, God, didn't want us to do, he'd turn to a page he had under our name and he'd write down what he did.

He had another book he wrote down the good things but he didn't spend too much time on that book. I guess because the preacher didn't think God got to use it much. He was always telling about the book with the sins in it and how God was always watching and could see even a bird when it died. So getting over on God was not something anyone could do according to him. If you sinned, you were caught. Bull.

Then, according to this preacher, when you died, he was going to turn to your page and read out all of your sins in front of everybody else and then send you to hell for it. Of course, if you hadn't done anything but good things, then he was going to let you into heaven where everything was going to be beautiful, with streets of gold and lots of people just like him.

Well, that didn't cut it with me, man. Still that thought of what goes around comes around crept into my mind.

That preacher kept saying how good God was but he didn't sound good to me. He sounded like a traffic cop hiding behind a billboard waiting to get you for speeding.

Besides, I had seen a lot of people, people who always did everything they were supposed to, have horrible things happen to them, like dying of cancer or being raped or losing all of their money or babies dying and if God was so good He sure wouldn't let that happen.

To top it all off, I didn't even believe there was a God anyway.

I didn't believe in anybody I couldn't see or hear or touch until after I died.

Then there was all of that talk about how good Christians were. Well, I had seen enough of them and read enough about them . . . killing each other in wars, torturing each other because one of them didn't believe exactly what the other said, going to court against each other because two bunches of them both said they owned the same building and they didn't want the other ones using it and on and on and on. I'd seen enough of them coming into jails I'd been in and looking down their noses at me and telling me how I better "get right" with their God. My God was a .38, clean and well oiled and a full safety-deposit box.

They'd ask me if I'd been saved. Saved for what? They were always talking about Jesus Christ. What could He do for me? I didn't see how somebody who lived about two thousand years ago and got himself hung up on a cross 'til he was dead for bucking the establishment could do anything for me.

Those three books I read in the Bible didn't say anything about him anyway. They were all about Abraham and Isaac and Jacob and Moses, mostly about Moses and how God got those people to do what He wanted them to do and what He told them not to do . . . so he could write it down in his bad book when they went ahead and did it anyway, I guess.

No, what I needed was something else. I needed to find out how to be the kind of guy I felt I was. I needed reality, not pie in the sky.

So the search went on. Day after day, week after week, month after month. Now Nietzsche, he appealed to me. He recognized that energy and pride and brains made a kind of superior guy who should really be put in the driver's seat. He drew a really great picture of what Christianity had done to the world. Yeah, I liked Nietzsche . . . yet, somehow, I had a funny kind of uneasiness about what he wanted, about the way he saw things.

I mean, I knew that what he was proposing wasn't possible, you can't wind the clock back, turn the calendar back to some time you like and start over there. I needed a now thing.

I began to read other people, novelists, playwrights, some biographies. Graves, Taylor Caldwell, Victor Hugo, Shaw.

Then one day, I read something from Shaw, I think, that was talking about the old Greek gods. These gods were looking down from Olympus at two armies fighting, the Spartans and the Athenians, I think. One of the minor deities said to Zeus, the head god, "Why are they fighting?" Zeus replied, "Because they want peace." And this minor god said, "Would they but look within."

Now it didn't hit me right then, but in a day or two this quotation began to come back to me.

"Would they but look within."

That I had been looking for some kind of peace, I knew. Where it was to be found, I did not know. I for sure hadn't found it in the books I had been reading although they had brought me to an awareness of vast areas of thought and concept far beyond and outside myself. I now began to understand that I wasn't going to find peace out there, though. If I was going to find it, it was going to have to be something that started inside of me.

A man who was at peace with himself, I saw, would be a man who would be . . . externally . . . exactly the same as he would be internally.

That night in my bunk that inner voice began again . . .

Your problem, Frank, is that you are really two different people. That's why you are so disillusioned about what you see yourself as having been, as being, because the outside guy's actions don't match the way the inside guy believes.

. . . and I knew this was right. I was divided. My mask was a projection of what I thought I ought to be or wanted to be. The job of making who I was conform to what I thought I ought to be, instead of letting who I was show in the way I acted, of letting what I did be an extension of who I was, had turned me around so much I didn't really know who I was.

In another lightning flash, though, there was one thing I did know. I knew that the self-invented projection of who I wanted to be . . . that Frank Costantino who I showed to all the world . . . was really who I was, what I was . . . a phoney.

That hurt. It hurt badly. Lying there on the bunk, I shook my shoulders as if, like a fly, I could shake the thought away by rippling my shoulder muscles.

I got up, right there in the middle of the night, and I wrote a poem. I can't remember all of it but I can remember enough of it to show where I was right then.

"Unhappy, restless, this you can see,
Though everything seen as you want it to be,
Fulfillment's evasive, peace wasn't there,
Yet, seek the answer, whose duty to care . . .
I can't remember the next part, but it went on . . .
"The horse of Troy is not what you seek
Illusion's no friend, it can't make you complete.
Pretend? Evade? Lead a life of despair.
Because fear of rejection will not let you dare
To reach out and take from life what is real
And know, and live the things that you feel?"

. . . and I knew I had a choice. *Be exactly externally what you are internally or pretend that you are not who you are . . . be a phoney.*

I want to be on the outside what I am on the inside!

Lying to yourself is a fool's kind of justification. Justification by deception doesn't do anything.

I can see that now. I can see my goals changing.

In another of those lightning fast glimmers, I saw that everybody had a way in which they dealt with who they were. Some of the guys around me were justifying their actions by comparing themselves to others who they thought were inferior to them. I had done the same thing when I compared myself to sex-offenders and to guards.

In that same glimmer I saw other guys trying to justify themselves by resorting to dope or booze until they were high enough to see themselves as they wanted to be.

One thing came through the flash. Escape through any means couldn't be the answer. The answer is in the truth. If you can know the truth you can see the way.

. . . and I began to look at myself and at everything I had ever done. It was funny, I had it all compartmentalized in my memory. The events of my life were like freight cars, lined up on a track stretching off beyond the horizon of my mind, each one filled with all of the incidents of a particular event . . . my Navy years, the eighteen months I was a professional wrestler, the year I got out of the Navy, robbing phone booths, marrying Bunny, the time I tried to kill a guy who stole some swag I had, a diamond robbery, a warehouse robbery and more and more and more . . . and the engine that pulled them all was that very macho, cool Frank Costantino.

The train ran all through the night.

13

In the months that followed a lot of things happened, yet they were all the kind of static things that happen within prisons, they didn't affect the real world.

This guy came in, that guy was transferred, that guy got killed, this guy went home, this guard retired, maybe a better one, maybe a worse one took his place.

Bunny came to see me, Bunny didn't come to see me, I was going to get transferred, I wasn't going to get transferred.

But day after day after day after day the walls stayed just as cold, the iron bars just as hard, the fear and hostility smelled just as musky as it had a day ago, a week ago, a month ago, a year ago.

I played poker in the same place, just the faces changed. I worked in the same kitchen, just the faces changed.

I used to wonder if any of them had ever seen themselves as walking through a crowd of people who stared at them . . . unseeing.

My nights began to be filled with those box cars coming out of nowhere and wheeling slowly into nothingness, each with its own event, its own case of me being the pusher . . . and those cars, as they went from rail to rail, didn't say, "clickety clack, clickety clack." They said, "You're just like them, Frank, just like them."

The clang of my cell door as it shut each night was like another sentence, a sentence to another night of isolation where I would be at the mercy of the struggle going on within my mind, between what I was and what some part of me wanted me to be.

Try as I might, I couldn't get away from the struggle. When they had told me about the fact that it was really my environment that was the root of my "problem," I hadn't even known that I had one except that I was in prison. Some other guy had told me that I was genetically unique and that was my problem . . . there wasn't another human being in the world who was exactly like me. So if it wasn't my fault, why was I suddenly wanting to be different? Huh???

Well, it hadn't been so sudden. It had come on slowly and was gaining momentum and every now and then I had to jerk myself back to reality and grab onto the fact that it wasn't my fault, to keep myself from flipping.

What I really needed, it dawned on me one night, was justice. My case cried for it. Cried out in the long reaches of the night for justice to be done for Frank.

How it was to be done, I didn't know, but I knew that I needed justice. I needed some way to have the cold terror and wrenching hurt of those days in the orphanage mended. I needed to have that "your mother doesn't want you," burned from my history.

If I wasn't responsible, I needed to have the past repaired, to have wrong righted, So much that was wrong had been done to me in the aloneness I felt day by day in this prison.

Justice, I want justice!

As I explored the countless paths that justice could take for me, I began to be conscious that they were all through narrow canyons, crevices, and valleys in the architecture of my past and above them loomed some great darkness, some great threatening mass.

As I would try justice on, stretched across the safety of my prison bunk, this mass, this turmoil above me would shift and change but never let me enjoy my imagined day when all the wrongs done on me were righted.

Yet, I couldn't put a name to it, I couldn't call it out and look at it. I could only know that it was kin to that spirit of uneasiness that had come to live within my cell.

Again one night, I heard myself scream "Justice!" Scream it out as if by hurling that word at it I could destroy that gloomy threat.

It woke me and as it did, that now persistent voice within me was speaking again.

Justice, Frank? Justice for whom?

For me, for me!

Justice for the robbed, Frank? Justice for the dead, Frank? Justice for the intimidated, Frank? For those whose dignity you've reduced?

No! For me, for me!

But Frank, justice for you includes justice for what you have done to others as well as for what has been done to you.

I knew what the dark cloud was. It was the cost to me, what I'd have to pay for.

Fear flooded through my body. It engulfed me in an instant. If I had to really pay for all those box cars of incidents . . . if I had to receive all of the intimidation that I had caused to everyone else, if I had to suffer through it here as the guards doled it out . . .

Nawh! Nawh! It wasn't like that. There wasn't any way they could even know about it all. Besides, I'm different. I wasn't like most guys, I was different. I'm still different.

No, I thought, I don't want justice. No, justice is the wrong thing . . . I couldn't pay the price of justice . . . well, I didn't want to, not just to get my own back . . . and that wouldn't be enough anyway.

No, I've done too much to people to such a degree that if I were to receive justice, I would have happen to me what I've done to other people.

Then something happened which changed the intensity of the pressure I was beginning to feel, the fear of somehow having to pay for all of what I had been, of what I was. It was a nebulous fear, like quick-silver that scatters on a table top from a broken thermometer. I couldn't get my hands on it and when I tried, it would break into a hundred little pieces and scatter through my mind. I had to do people right.

One day when I was over at The Rock to see the doctor, two guys came looking for me and they were there waiting for me when I came out. They were in trouble, bad trouble, and they needed help fast. They knew I had some connections in the place and had access to more.

One of the guys, a guy named Bad Eye Eddie, who I'd known on the street, came across this guy in the chow line one day he'd known on the street. He hadn't known him well, but knew him well enough to know two things.

One, he shouldn't ever have been sent to prison

anywhere. He was a real innocent. Not quite bright enough to ever get in real trouble and too dumb not to be used.

Two, the kid was scared to death.

So Bad Eye spoke to him and asked him how he was doing and kind of tried to let him know he would be a friend.

When he did, the kid turned around and looked at him and his eyes began to water and a tear ran down his cheek and the kid's legs start to shaking and Bad Eye realized the kid was terrified of something.

He's a good looking kid, and Bad Eye puts his arm on his shoulder, and says, "Hey, hey, kid, what's wrong?"

Then this kid blurted out this story.

It seems that a bunch of guys on the kitchen crew had gotten him after breakfast that day. They had just suddenly appeared as he was leaving the hall and stood around him so he couldn't get past them.

Then one of them had grabbed him, not too rough, but so he couldn't swing away, by the throat, and said, "Sonny boy, you're our meat. We're going to teach you some things about sex you never dreamed of. You're going to have so much fun, you just won't know what hit you. Now, if you don't want to get hurt, hurt bad, I mean like maybe never getting up again, you're going to meet us after chow tonight right here behind the mess hall."

"The hell I will," the kid stuttered out and the big guy just tightened his fist at the kid's throat for a couple of seconds and the kid began to wilt.

"Just remember, kid, you will. There ain't no place in this joint we can't get to you. You be there, at six tonight."

Well, the kid said okay he would. All morning the

fear had been building up in him and now he couldn't even eat his lunch.

So now, Bad Eye's saying to me, "I know about these guys. This kid needs help to stop them."

"Okay," I said, "stay put till I get back in touch with you. I'll need some help but let me see if I can get some protection spread over you."

I got in touch with an old partner of mine in The Rock and told him the problem.

When I came back to tell them they were okay, that a patch was made, I was feeling pretty good. You haven't lost your power, Frank, see? Even in here, man, you can still get things done.

Then I told them and Bad Eye thanks me and this kid says do you know what this kid says? He says, "Thank God."

Well, God didn't have a thing to do with it. It was me and my pals. Well, I thought, so much for you kid, and I went out into the yard.

God! Well, there wasn't any God. I stood under this tree in the yard kicking the dirt around and thinking about the injustice of it all. Here I used all of my clout, with my friends, my connections, to protect this dumb kid and what does he do? He thanks God!

I looked down and ants were scurrying away from my foot and I thought, "They probably think I'm God."

A termite was edging away from a weed toward the ant hill and furious activity began to take place with the ants. I could just hear them.

This one little ant looks up to me and says, "Oh God!"

Because I'm big and he thought I was God, see?

"Oh, God," he said, "if you would just reach your

big foot over there, you could stomp that termite and we wouldn't have to go to war."

I looked down.

"Ain't going to though."

"Ohhhhh, God, I beseech you!"

"Talk a little louder. Beseech me a little more."

The little ants started running around and they're all getting ready to defend their nest and then here comes this beetle from the other side and now they're really in confusion.

The beetle got the little ant who was the beseecher.

Then his little ant-wife started crying, "Ohhh, my husband, my husband, my husband!"

I just stood there.

"Oh God, help us!"

"You ain't talking loud enough."

Then the beetle got right on top of the ant hill and was really wreaking havoc and the ant-wife was screaming, "Oh, God!"

Then I lifted my foot and stomped on the beetle and ants and the whole thing. One stomp and it was all destroyed.

I walked away. Dumb ants. There ain't no God . . .

Nothing's real. It's all just a big joke. That's what it is, a big joke.

That same afternoon, one of those guys who had been after Bad Eye's friend, was out on the weight pile pumping iron. He's just gotten a couple of hundred pounds up above his head when some other young kid he'd been screwing around with came up behind him and drove a ten inch piece of steel right through his kidney. Then he stabbed the guy and stabbed him and stabbed him until he was dead.

Unh hunh, I thought, what goes around comes around.

That night on my bunk as the loneliness crept along the corridor outside my cell, one phrase washed up from the violence I had heard that day. One phrase and it was like a piece of driftwood trying to wash up on the beach at ebb tide that goes out with each wave but comes right back in the next . . . what goes around comes around . . . what goes around comes around . . . what goes around comes around.

I'd seen happen it so many times. The thief who got robbed. The jock whose wife was stepping out on him. The hit man with the bullet through the back of his head.

. . . what goes around comes around . . .

I closed my eyes and fought the feeling of hopelessness that was beginning to engulf me.

Regret quietly crawled into the bunk with me and as it did, that freight train of guilt came rattling down the road of my memory, dragging behind it a lifetime of freight, car after car after car after car. I thought, oh if I could only have a second chance.

A long, sad "ohhhhhhh" escaped my lips and I didn't know whether it was the freight train blowing or just me sighing . . . I guess they were both the same sound.

Part II

. . . but he that soweth to the Spirit
shall of the Spirit reap life everlasting.

Galatians 6:8

14

One day I was told I was moving. I went a little different from the guy who had first ridden the Gray Ghost from Miami to Raiford. I had some more knowledge. I knew a little bit more of what depraved men would do to one another.

I knew that all of those writers I had read had never really found an answer . . . they had just laid out a system or something which they thought would lead to an answer, maybe, if you followed their plan. It seemed the only reality was that, reality was unattainable to the mind of man.

I knew I wasn't really, finally, responsible for what I had done, that it was my environment, my genes, that had landed me in prison. After all I had no control over either.

. . . and I knew one other thing.

I knew that it was all a joke, life was. Fifty years from now, what difference would it make?

We got to Glades and we had to go through another indoctrination program so we would know what they thought they were doing at that prison. Part of the indoctrination course was a talk by the prison chaplain.

It had been ten years since that newspaper reporter first called me "sophisticated" after that Boston robbery. I had eight more years of crime and two years of Raiford since then so I knew what the joke was when I went into that chapel to hear Max Jones.

Now Glades Correctional Institution is in farming country. They call it "The Muck." Flat as a pancake as far as you can see and everything that's not planted in vegetables is planted in sugar cane. They grew and canned most of the vegetables eaten in the Florida prison system at Glades.

When we got to the chapel, this big country preacher came out and started telling us jokes. He looked like he had just come in from Tennessee . . . and his jokes sounded like he had heard them up there. Well, maybe they weren't jokes, maybe he was just trying to talk to us. Anyway they weren't funny, though a lot of the guys laughed. He must have talked for ten minutes just saying things like, "Fellows, if I can't help you, I won't hurt you!"

Then he'd laugh and some of the guys would laugh a little and he would say something else, like: "If you all come to church on Sunday and you don't like the sermon, I'll give you back everything you put in the plate, ha! ha!"

This went on and on and I couldn't wait for him to finish and let us get out of there. Then, right in the middle of his bad jokes, he stopped dead still and kind of a change came over him.

I mean he just changed right there in front of my eyes. He was a big guy anyway, and where before he had looked sort of unassuming . . . well, not unassuming, unchallenging is the word, I guess . . . all of a sudden he was a man of authority.

It wasn't that he had begun talking different because he hadn't said a word yet since he stopped talking. In a real quiet way he began to look at us, right in the eye and I had never had anybody look at me that way. I just sensed this guy liked me. Just the way he looked at me made me know, somehow, he saw me. I can't explain it. I had never felt like that with anybody before. I knew I liked him. I couldn't figure it out. The only thing I knew about this guy was that he told jokes, yet I knew I liked him and, more than that, I wanted to sit down and talk with him.

I couldn't think of any way to do that, though. I didn't see the Chaplain playing poker with us and I, for sure, wasn't going to come to chapel so I could be around him.

All of this probably didn't last more than a couple of seconds and then he said, "Men, I've got something that I want to share with you."

The funny thing about that was that I knew from the way he was acting that he did and, what's more, I wanted him to share it.

"I want you to know that if you are in trouble or if you have a need, I am here. That's what I'm here for and I want you to come to me."

Hot stuff! Same garbage. Disappointment flooded through me. It was a real let down. I didn't have any needs I couldn't answer myself and I wasn't about to go to a chaplain with it if one did turn up. The way I saw it, that'd be in the same boat with going to a policeman if somebody was giving you trouble.

Somehow, though, in spite of the anger and the let down, I couldn't shake the pull I felt toward Max Jones.

"I want to share with you a word of testimony before you leave here today," he added. It wasn't any long thing, no bunch of background, not a lot of high-sounding theology.

"Men," he said, "one day after I had done a lot of living, I found myself going out to a revival meeting. That preacher didn't have a whole lot of fancy equipment. He just had an old tent, lots of folding chairs, a little platform about the size of a truck bed and an upright piano . . . and the Word of God.

"As he began to talk, I began to look back over my life and I found out there was a whole lot of things in my life that I'd done wrong that I'd now rather not have done at all and I started trying to figure out a way to undo them.

"I figured and figured and figured and you know what? There just wasn't any way I could do anything at all about any of it. I don't think I have ever felt as helpless, no, nor as hopeless in my life as I did that night.

"It just seemed like the bottom fell right out of everything that was holding my spirits up and I just sank and sank and sank until I couldn't sink any lower and then I got up and went up to the altar. He didn't really have any altar, he just had an old chair with a throw-cover over it.

"Anyway, I went up there and I asked Jesus to come into my life. My wife accepted Christ the same night at the same chair and He's never left me since and, man, I want to tell you, each of us will stand accountable to God.

"Somehow or another, men, each of you has got to come to the place where you decide about your life, and the price you will have to pay if you die without Christ."

. . . and deep inside of me a jumble of words and phrases from the past were swirling up into my head

. . . "You're just like them, Frank, you take what you want, you always have" . . . "What goes around comes around" . . . "Phoney" . . . and I caught a glimpse of that freight train, or maybe I just heard it.

He went on, about Jesus Christ, God's own Son, and how He'd come down here among us as a man and agreed to pay that debt we could never pay, how He was bruised for our iniquities, how He was wounded for our transgressions, and by His stripes we were healed. He was quoting the Bible and he really believed what he said.

"Men," he said, "Jesus paid the price for your sins because the price for sins was greater than any man could pay. If you ask Him into your life, He will come in. He came into my life that night and anything that's good in me, anything that is alive, anything that is likable in me is Jesus Christ in me.

"I know that I know that I know that Jesus Christ is my personal Saviour."

. . . . and I was thinking, he's right, he's right, that's it! Then I suddenly became aware of what I was thinking. Bull! What does this clown think he is talking about?

I knew it was all a joke. A big empty nothing. What was I doing, about to let this guy sucker me into this stuff?

I am the captain of my ship and the master of my fate! He went on with the rest of the spill about if we needed to talk to come see him, he was in the chapel every day except Friday and Saturday. It would be a cold day, I thought. Anyway, he was through and we got out of there.

The days passed and the anger inside me was building to a fever pitch. (In fact, the prison experience had taken its toll on me.) I was in a new prison and that, in a sense, meant starting all over, only I wasn't into starting over.

I was into blowing up. Anytime I felt someone pushing I'd bristle. Even little unsignificant things like someone cutting in the chow line affected me personally and the anger would build.

I lived in a dorm with two hundred men, a hundred on each side of an open day room which consisted of benches and a television set on the wall. The TV was a constant source of tension because of the jaw-jacking during programs and the decisions that had to be made over the choice of which program to watch.

A hundred guys and one TV is a situation with an infinite number of explosions possible in it. Anyway, there's this little bunch of guys in the dorm playing strong-arm and they've got these dumb shows they like to watch and nobody else gets to see anything they want to see. We were supposed to vote on what station to watch but they had a deal worked up where they had a bunch of guys who didn't care what was on because they were going to be doing something else and they'd all come up and vote with their buddies, then after the vote they'd truck off to play poker or whatever.

Or, worse still, they'd get a bunch of their buddies in there and then change a channel right in the middle of a program we'd voted to watch just because they didn't like what was happening.

Well, I decided there had been too much of that. I knew that if I was watching a show and one of those touch-hogs got up and changed the channel his butt was mine.

It happened. I was watching a show and this jitterbug comes and changes the channel.

I got up without going into the thing and went to my sack.

The next night I went to my stash and got my piece. It was about 14 inches long and sharp. I kept it handy in the dorm.

In the day room those guys knew something was up. They just didn't know what. The air was filled with it.

There was a show at eight that a bunch of us wanted to see and sure enough, when the break came at eight, all these turkeys came pouring in and voted to see some other stupid show. As soon as they'd voted, they all trooped out again.

When they were gone, I got up and walked up to the TV and just switched it to the channel we wanted to watch. Then, as I was going back to where I was sitting, this big guy unfolds himself, real slow, as if I was a kid and hadn't realized what I was doing, and walks up to the TV and starts to reach for the knob.

I said, "Don't touch that knob." The tone of my voice spun him around. I could feel my heart racing as the adrenaline began to run. The blood was pounding in my temples and I could taste it in my mouth . . . the blood taste. I let the piece drop down into my hand from my sleeve. It glistened in the silvery light of the TV.

The tension was thick enough to cut. I looked straight at the touch-hog. It was his move and he knew it. Was he prepared to die? No. I saw it in his eyes. He wanted a way out without looking bad.

One of his friends back behind him in the darkness somewhere said, "Don't let that sucker back you down, man."

I turned to the guy in the back and said, "Sucker? Well, boy," and I emphasized the 'boy', "don't ask him to climb no tree you ain't willing to climb yourself."

He started grumbling something and walked away. The crisis was over. There wasn't going to be any killing.

Somebody in the back said "the heats coming," and here came a guard. The crowd broke up. There was some talking to some guys but nobody said anything then. Tomorrow some rat would fill the man's ear.

I wasn't so concerned about the trip to the captain's office, which came the next morning, as I was with the fact that I had in reality acted very stupidly over a very stupid thing. The time was getting to me. I was changing and I didn't like it. Life sucked and all I could think was, screw the world, the whole stinking world.

That night as I was going to sleep, I kept thinking about Max Jones, and about what he had said. It kept coming back to me. Was it possible that there could be an answer and that he, Max Jones, had it? He said he did and he sounded so sure. That's why he had interested me, almost captured me.

All that stuff about Jesus I had heard before. I could see Jesus was a giver not a taker. That in itself was unusual. Givers weren't usually famous people, just the takers achieved fame most of the time. Yet, Jesus was famous, and he was a giver. I worried that around for a while and finally slept.

For duty at Glades, I was a house-man and worked in a dormitory. That was good duty. I didn't have a lot to do. It gave me a lot of free time. Too much time, so I started into physical fitness on the iron pile. I would build part of this time with the iron, but still there was time, plenty of time to think and at night, too. I began again to plan an escape. It wasn't going to be so hard to do from here. Bunny was coming up every weekend now and I could get away from this area easy.

At night, though, when I stretched out to go to sleep, when I shut my eyes, I didn't see a picture of me shagging down the road to a perfect escape. No, I saw Max Jones standing up there saying, "I know that I know that I know that Jesus Christ is my personal Saviour."

How did he know that anyway?

That freight train kept coming around the bend in my mind, whistle blowing mournful and lonesome, as everyone else slept. Waking in the still, blind alleys of my nights, I would hear, echoing across the void of sleep as if someone had just said it before I came in, Charlie's voice saying, "You're just like them, Frank. You're a taker, Frank. You take what you want, Frank."

I'd squint my eyes and look back through the edges of wakefulness into my sleep and there would be those five guys dancing and swaying around that kid's bunk.

"You're just like them, Frank."

I tried every trick I had ever heard of to shut out the echoes of that voice, to derail that train, to melt the image of those guys around that kid's bunk. Nothing worked. If anything, it got worse, day by day.

Was I flipping out? Had I stood too many counts? Nawh! You can't get institutionalized in two years! I'd only been in two years. It seemed like forever. Like I'd never been free, like freedom was a dream—something that had never been. Maybe I was dead and this was really hell I was in?

Stop it, man! You'll flip completely. Something inside me said, "You'll flip!"

I thought, "Man, you have flipped!"

All of this guilt, talking to turnips and ants. It *was* hell. . . . a feeling of frustration came over me, a helplessness born of desperation. If I wasn't dead, I ought to be.

I walked out of the front door of the dorm and went over to the chapel looking for Max Jones. When I got over there, though, I suddenly asked myself what I was going to say to him.

I couldn't think of anything to say, I couldn't think of a question to ask him that didn't sound either stupid or fake. There I was, standing around in front of the chapel trying to make up my mind what to do and then I began to wonder what I looked like hanging around out there so I just turned around and went back to the dorm.

During the next week or so, I must have gone over there six or eight times to that chapel, then turned around and come back to the dorm without going in.

. . . and every night I was hearing that voice talk to me about owing a debt I couldn't pay.

Finally, one morning, I went over to the chapel, walked up the steps and right past a couple of guys who were sitting at a table by the door reading and went back into the right hand corner of the room where a door opened into the Chaplain's office. I knocked on the door.

"Come in," he said.

I did and there I stood confronting this guy whose words had been eating away at me for almost 2 months . . . "I know, that I know, that I know that Jesus Christ is my personal Saviour."

He stood up and stuck his hand out to me and said, "I'm Chaplain Jones. Come on in and sit down."

"My name's Frank Costantino," I said, "and I've got some questions I want to ask you." I sat down and he sat down. His desk was sort of cluttered up and he fished some stuff out of one of the drawers and said, "Okay, ask away. Will you have a cup of coffee?"

"Yeah thanks," I said, and that kind of threw me because I hadn't expected anybody in a staff uniform in a prison to offer to drink coffee with me.

After he had given me the coffee, he pulled his chair around beside the desk so there wasn't anything between us except an old carpet on the floor and said, "What's on your mind, Frank?"

I didn't know where to begin so I started talking about the trip I was on to find out who I was and why I was. Finally I was talking to him about how I was trying to find out where I was going and how my life fit into life in a total sense.

"I've been reading a lot, a lot of philosophy and other stuff and don't see where they ever got it all together. I just want to know where you got to be convinced about Jesus Christ so that you know that you know that you know that He's your Saviour?"

As soon as I finished, I knew I had sounded like I was ready to fight but there wasn't anything I could do about that. Anyway, he didn't pay any attention to it.

He said, "Truth is a person and the person you're looking for is Jesus." That stopped me cold. He went on to say that what I was looking for was God and he told me about who He was and said that finding Him wasn't possible through intellectual assent.

"The people who were building the tower of Babel," he said, "were trying to reach God through their own strength and their tower was as ridiculous as man's attempts to find the truth because God and the truth were one and the same. The only way a man can find truth is to find God, and where would he begin to look for God?"

As I listened to him, some of the words he used somehow got translated in my mind into direct questions I had. It was sort of like him speaking in one language and me hearing in another language that was speaking right to my internal self.

I really understood somehow that God must be outside of all that had been created and that He was not a part of creation, but rather creation was a part of Him and again the vastness of the whole thing smothered my mind.

Someone outside of creation? If that's the case, how can men find God? And, if God is truth, how can men see more than vague shadows of the reality they so desparately seek?

The clerk brought the coffee in and that broke my trend of thought. We drank from the cups and had some small talk and then Max said something to the effect that God as a loving father desired to be reunited with his creation.

What I thought, and then said was, "How do you know that?"

He turned to the Bible and started to quote some scriptures: "Behold I stand at the door and knock and if any man hear my voice and will open the door, I will come in and sup with him and he with me."

He said, "God knew man could not find Him or

reach Him and so he came into the world as a man and that man is Jesus."

He said that Jesus was not just a man but was also God and that it was through Jesus that man and God could be reconciled.

He went on to talk about the purpose for the death of Jesus Christ and that in His death He paid a price he didn't owe because each of us owed a debt we couldn't pay. That struck a cord inside me again, that language inside me that caused me to understand something I couldn't absorb mentally . . . and again my thoughts started to wander.

If what Max Jones was saying was true, then could that mean that Jesus was indeed willing to stand in my place and receive my justice for me? Stand in my stead and reap the crop I planted?

It seemed right that there must be a plan . . . a plan that applied to everything, which held everything, all matter, together. Hadn't I read somewhere that nothing is solid but that objects are really molecular masses of different densities?

I remember at the time thinking that I, being one molecular mass, theoretically, could pass through the bars that were holding me in because the bars were another such mass and there was all sorts of space between the molecules. I wondered if that's how Jesus had walked on the water. Did he change the molecular structure of the water, probably not . . . He probably changed his structure . . . that is if He walked on water at all. Still there has to be a force greater than what is seen.

I must know this unless I had an imagination big enough to imagine that the whole universe, with all of its laws like gravity and like seeds will always produce the same thing they came from and the stars will always do the same things, unless I imagined that all of that was an accident. That didn't really make much sense. If you put nothing together with nothing you get nothing.

There was a plan for everything, he said, like in an acorn there was a plan inside it to be an oak tree, a certain kind of oak tree, to grow a certain way and I knew that was true. Was it the same way with us? Did God have such a plan for us? I, somehow, knew He did.

My mind came back to what Max was saying. It seemed as though he was saying that there was only one way to this central truth. He said that Jesus Christ, who was not just a man but was also God, had come along and made it possible for us to get out of the mess we had gotten ourselves into.

Then he told me that Jesus had died for me, personally, to pay for my sins, so I wouldn't have to pay for them. He said, Jesus had known me, who I was and what I was going to be like.

In spite of knowing all of that about me, he said Jesus loved me enough to get up on that cross and suffer all of that shame and agony, all of that degradation so that I could get out of where I was if I wanted to get out.

"All of that," he said, "was God's way of doing for us what we couldn't do for ourselves . . . reach Him. Christ was God's way of showing us His truth," or at least that's what I understood him to say.

He said, "Frank, Jesus is the truth. What you're really looking for is a personal relationship with Jesus Christ." It was funny. I didn't really understand what he was talking about but I knew that whatever it was, he was right.

I didn't know how to describe, even to myself,

what was happening in my head and my heart. I was hearing one thing, with my ears, hearing Max say something that I didn't really comprehend as applying to me. Yet somewhere inside of me, my heart was being changed, and I was reacting to a different message. I was suddenly coming into possession of truths which I hadn't gotten either by reading or hearing.

It meant something in the very heart of my being though I didn't know what. I thought, it fits. It's right. All I could think about was, how in the world, could I have a personal relationship with somebody who died two thousand years ago?

I didn't say any of that though. I just dead-panned him. You know? I looked at him with that "I'm with you" look.

You know the look. You see it on a lot of people. They've always got that, "Oh, yes, I know. You're quite right," smile on their face. They sit there and smile and smile in all of their hurt until their teeth dry up.

He was going on, talking about what life with His Lord and Saviour, Jesus Christ, was like. He said that Jesus is very much alive, that He rose again and is ruling now.

"He is risen," he said.

I'd heard the words before but they never struck the cord they did now.

He is risen . . . He's alive?

"Frank," he said, "Jesus is active in your life right here in this office right now."

. . . and I smiled on and my teeth dried out. Pride. Old pride. Pride wouldn't let me say, "Hey, man, I'm hurting."

Do you know what he finally said to me? Right

out of the blue he said, "Frank, before you go, I'd like to pray with you."

I was too embarrassed to say no. I looked down at the floor to keep from looking into those eyes of his and he took that for a signal and began to pray.

I don't remember how he started off but I remember thinking, he's talking to God like He's right here in the room with us. I remember him saying something like . . . "Jesus, Frank's looking for the truth, for something real and he needs to see who the truth is, that it's You, Lord, he's looking for.

"He doesn't want this life he's had . . . that's easy to see."

Max had summarized right where I was in a single statement and I flashed back on the life I had had and didn't want. I looked back on that life filled with its hurts and its pains. The full impact of my sin descended upon me and I felt the weight of it pressing down upon me. I remembered thinking and perhaps saying, there ain't no way Jesus is going to do anything for me. I've done too much . . .

Max went on to tell me about Paul the Apostle and how he had murdered the early followers of Christ, and how God not only forgave him but used him to preach the Gospel to the lost.

"Do you understand Frank?" Max said "Jesus is waiting for you right now and if you'll ask Him into your life He'll come in and give you what you're looking for."

. . . and I knew it was all true. The words began to form in my mind. In desperation, I thought: God is it true? Do you care for me? Do you want me? . . .

Right then I was aware that this great kind of peace and quiet was beginning to pour down around my shoulders and surround me and I knew I was face to face with God, even if I didn't understand Him and couldn't see Him. I knew I was going to ask Him and I was afraid He would get away before I could do it.

I didn't know how I was going to say it or what I was going to say, but I knew I was going to ask God to take over my life and I knew He was going to do it.

Max began to pray again. He said, "Father, reveal to Frank your Son. Father reveal to him who Jesus is. Father let him know that every hair on his head is numbered. Father, let him know that you love him today, just as he is because you already see him as he is going to be. Father, speak to Frank. Show him that what he's really looking for is your forgiveness, your gift of grace and love, Jesus Christ."

I'd never heard anybody pray like that. I'd never had anybody ask God, "Show him . . ." God was right there in that little chapel office and I knew it. Max knew it and he also knew me. I'd never had anybody really recognize my hurt before.

It was funny. One minute, I couldn't pray. I didn't even know how to go about talking to God in His heaven. The next minute, God was in that room with me and I knew He was somebody I could talk to. I could feel His presence.

"God," I said, "I hurt. If you care for me and want me, knowing what I've been and what I am, then take my life. I don't want it like it is."

I couldn't understand that Jesus might want my life at all. I could hardly look at it myself by now. I began to recount my life to Him. The freight train came out of the mists and I described each car's contents to him as it came in sight and it was a long time before I became aware that as the cars were being hauled away, they were empty.

It was October 21, 1969, and I bear witness that on that day heaven came down and glory filled my soul . . .

The Son of God came into my life and I knew Jesus Christ.

The Spirit of God purged me and I knew the Holy Spirit was present in me, cleansing me and I began to cry and it seemed the most normal thing in the world.

I wasn't sobbing, I was just leaking. My shirt was getting wet and I heard myself saying, "Oh, my God, my God! How could I have been so stupid? How could I have been so wrong? How could I have been so dumb? So empty?"

. . . and the Lord my God, my Father in heaven, began to heal me right there in that little room. I don't really know how long I was down there on my knees with Max Jones, but I knew that when I was through and I stood up and looked at Max, still down there on his knees in the middle of the floor, when I stood there in that shirt wet with tears, I was a born-again son of God, a child of the king and an heir to the Kingdom of Heaven.

I remembered that I would have settled for a second chance at life if someone had given it to me. For months, I had just been saying, "Oh, if only I had a second chance . . ."

But God didn't give me a second chance, he gave me a new life.

. . . and I have never, in the quiet corners of the night, heard Charlie's voice again, nor have I seen that freight train coming around the bend of my mind.

As I walked out of that chapel, I was still in man's prison, but the prison I had been born in was gone and I walked out into a free place where God's peace reigns . . .

Part III

And let us not be weary in well doing;
for in due season we shall reap, if we faint not.
As we have therefore opportunity,
let us do good unto all men,
especially unto them who are of the household of God.

Galatians 6:9-10

15

As I was walking back to the dorm, wave after wave of gratitude washed over me, lifting me and floating me along in an eddy of God's grace as I moved through the noonday flow of grumbling inmates on their way to chow.

I had a new life and I knew it. I thought how great God was. He hadn't "modified my behavior," He had given me a new life . . . rebirth. It's strange how I knew that so perfectly. I was reborn, the concept became a living reality.

The world had been trying to restore me to my original self but God had said no. I'm not an ex-anything!

He took that old life, that freight train, and just held it up in front of me, car by car, act by act, piece by piece, person by person . . . and as I said, "Lord, I'm sorry," He let it die.

Walking along, I suddenly knew that when that old life died, back there in Max Jones' office, God buried it, forever and ever. Jesus Christ had died and was risen, so that I could be risen in new birth. He had taken my sins and they were hidden in Him now for all time.

I felt as if the world had been lifted off of my shoulders and I knew I was the tallest man in the world right then as I felt my spirit soaring high above the currents of time and space and somehow touching the eternal heart of God. I didn't know how this could be. It was beyond my understanding but, still, I knew it was so.

Back in the dorm, I stretched out on my bunk and experienced my second prayer that was really "alive," one where I knew someone was listening, and I started thanking God for what He had done for me.

Max Jones had given me a Bible when I left the chapel and I opened it. For a moment I thought of reading it from start to finish, but then thought I'd better start reading in the book of John in the New Testament like he had told me. St. John, he said, declares the divinity of Jesus. He tells who Jesus is, the other gospels tell what He did.

I read and read and I couldn't get enough of it. I had a hunger for that Bible. When I finished John, I went on and read the book of Acts, then I went back and read Matthew, Mark and Luke.

Bunny was coming to see me Sunday, so I couldn't go to chapel. I went out and waited where I could look up the road to where visitor's cars turned the corner, waiting for Bunny to come so I could tell her what had happened to me. I wondered what her reaction would be and how I was going to tell her.

When I saw the car, I headed toward the fence and waited for a visitor's call-out. You couldn't meet your visitors as they came in. They had to sign-in and tell the guard who they were visiting. The guard then had to give the name to an inmate runner who in turn would tell you that you had a visitor.

The list of what you could do and couldn't do about visitors was 13 pages long and was called Visiting Regulations and Proceedures. It told you exactly what to do. For instance, under the item of general conduct, it said:

(1) Inmates who have been advised that they have visitors will report to the visiting park officer who will check the inmate into the park. Visits will be conducted in an orderly and acceptable manner. Petting and obscene mannersims will not be permitted.

(2) Dress code for inmates in the visiting park will be issued uniforms only.

(3) Inmates are not to give visitors any item to take out of the visiting park, except items authorized by the officer in charge.

(4) Upon completion of the visit, the inmate will immediately return to the visiting park officer and will not escort visitors to the Gatehouse. Also, visitors will not escort inmates to inner gate. Inmates will not stay in the visiting park and visit other persons not on his approved list after his visit is terminated.

(5) Inmates must declare all monies and personal possessions with the visiting park officer prior to entering the park and returning to the compound. Possession of funds in excess of the authorized amount will be in violation of Institution Regulations.

(6)Inmates not having visitors will not be permitted into the visiting park and will not be permitted to converse through the fence. Inmates will not congregate on the sidewalk or in the area adjacent to the visiting park.

(7) Visitors are cautioned that the introduction of weapons, narcotics, alcoholic beverages, or other unauthorized items onto State Correctional Institution property is a felony offense. (Florida

Statutes 944.43 and 944.47)

(8) Persons desiring to visit must be fully clothed and inmates are cautioned to advise their visitors accordingly. Hot pants, short shorts, and see-through blouses are not appropriate attire.

(9) No person will appear on the visiting list of two or more inmates except in the case of family relationship to the inmates involved.

(10) Visitors are not authorized to introduce cameras onto institutional property.

(11) Persons under the influence of alcoholic beverages or narcotics will not be allowed to visit nor will they be allowed on institutional property.

(12) Packages, food or gifts will not be permitted into the visiting park. Items purchased at the visiting park canteen by inmates or for inmates will be consumed in the visiting park prior to the visit termination.

(13) No item will be given directly to an inmate. (Exceptions: Cash in the amount which will not cause the inmate to exceed the maximum possession limit may be given to him. Denomination is not to exceed a $5.00 bill.)

And that's just about two and a half pages of that 13 pages.

When Bunny finally got there, I told her. I told her the whole thing and I thought she'd be excited. After all, she used to complain all the time about the way I lived, my friends, and occupation. She was always trying to get me to quit stealing and go straight, so I thought she'd really be happy about what had happened to me. I told her about my conversion and she just looked at me.

She was overwhelmed. As she began to talk to me about it, haltingly and kind of embarassed, I realized that, though she thought it was nice and though she had seen bits and pieces in me that had changed, she didn't really believe it would be a permanent thing.

When she was all through, I said, "Bunny, I am not only going to live differently, I am going to live better. This whole thing with Jesus is going to last because it's for real. God came down and he touched me . . . "

I could tell by the look on her face that she just didn't understand it.

We talked some more about it and I told her about what I had been reading in the Bible and everything, but I know she went home thinking it would all pass away in a few days or a few weeks or a few months.

When I got back to my bunk after she left, I took out my Bible and sat there a minute. I was really low. Bunny's reaction had really stung me. The full impact of where she was became a reality to me. I thought . . . Bunny knows who Jesus is, she just hasn't met Him, and there's a difference. I prayed for my wife for the first time . . .

After I finished talking to God, I opened the Bible and I began reading where I had stopped that morning. It was in Galatians, in chapter six. As I began to read verse seven, it was as if I was hearing the words aloud. I read words that were to be burned eternally in my soul.

"Be not deceived; God is not mocked; for whatsoever a man soweth, that shall he also reap."

"For he that soweth to his flesh shall of the flesh reap corruption . . . "

I knew as I read that , God was speaking directly to me. I just looked at the sum total of my life up to that moment on the floor in the chapel office and here I was in prison, huh? And I had gotten exactly what I deserved . . . because I had planted the garden I was walking in.

It was a garden where I'd planted hate and distrust, animosity, envy, bitterness and selfishness.

It was a garden in which no thanksgiving grew.

The pain, the loneliness, the anger, the emptiness, all of the things that had been surrounding me, I had been reaping. The garden had been in full bloom and I had been reaping the things that I had sowed.

My sin had literally borne fruit. The harvest had been in and my sin had been killing me.

Then Max Jones had come along and told me that Jesus said He would reap everything I had sowed . . . and I knew He had. I hadn't been able to understand that.

That Jesus Christ had come into my life, I knew because I could never forget when I was down on the floor on my knees in Max Jones' office I argued with myself about it but there was no way of arguing with what had happened, with the experience I had had.

I read on in Galatians.

". . . But he that soweth to the Spirit shall of the Spirit reap life everlasting . . . ."

. . . and I thought to myself, what goes around comes around. Hallelujah! Jesus Christ had set me free in a way I never believed possible. He had done it by giving me a new life to live. I had sowed to the Spirit on that floor in the chapel by confessing my sins and I was now, I knew, reaping life everlasting, because God had made a way for me.

The next Wednesday, I went to the mid-week service at the chapel, I remember getting kind of angry when I walked in there because there were only about 20 men in the chapel.

At some point in the sevice, Max Jones asked, "Does anybody here want to stand up for Jesus?"

A guy in the pew across the aisle from me got up and told about what had happened to him since he asked Jesus Christ to take over his life. Then a guy a couple of rows in front of me got up and told about his experiences with God.

They both talked for about five or ten minutes and it was all really interesting. I felt something urging me to get up, too, but I didn't have all that much to say. I mean, those two guys had been at this thing for a long time. One of them four months and one of them for four years and here I had only known the Lord for five days.

But I kept feeling like I was supposed to get up. So, I got up. I can't remember exactly what I said but I do know it must have been the shortest witness on record. It went something like this: "I don't have a lot to say," I said, "but I do want to say I have accepted Jesus Christ as my Saviour."

The chaplain had some coffee and we stood around after the service and talked with some of the men in the prison I'd never talked to before. I left there feeling more sure and certain about what had happened to me than I had anytime since I left the chaplain's office that day.

There were two guys I'd known a long time and saw a lot of, and I knew I had to tell them about what had happened to me. They knew something had happened and had already been asking what was up with me. One of them was Louie Matire and the other was Mike Sotola.

We used to walk around the big recreation field when we had some things we wanted to talk about, so a couple of mornings after I stood up in chapel that night, I said, "Lets go take a walk," and we went.

It was pretty hard trying to get started in what I wanted to tell them but I stumbled through it somehow. I really wasn't so sure about where I was at that moment because there were still many things which were uncertain to me. I didn't even fully understand the impact on me of my own experience.

As soon as I started talking about Jesus Christ they began to get edgy but I knew I had to tell them. What I really ended up doing was not so much witnessing about Jesus Christ as telling them about my own experience on the chapel floor that day.

I knew that a change had taken place in me, that I was, in fact, a new creature. I just didn't know how to tell them about it. They were polite. We had been friends for a long time. They didn't give me any jazz or anything. They just didn't believe me. They thought I was scamming, getting over on the preacher.

I finally gave up and said, "Let's go back in."

I couldn't understand it. I was so full of what had happened to me and wanted so much to share Jesus Christ with those closest to me and yet when I tried, with Bunny, with Louis, with Mike, they just turned off on me, didn't believe me.

I knew what had happened was real and I knew I was a new guy. Why wouldn't they believe me? Back at my bunk, I began to pray about it. I just said, "Father, what's wrong with me? Why won't they believe me? Why can't I make them believe me?"

I was really full of what had happened to me but now a new fear began to grow in me, fear that no one would ever believe me.

I reflected back on my inner journey, through mind darkness and mental blindness. I didn't know how this would line-up with Christian teaching or even philosophical thinking but what I knew was that for 28 years I had been blind to the reality of Christ. Sort of like driving a car with a blindfold, the faster you go the more damage you can cause, and I had it open full throttle.

Well that's where I had been. Blind and traveling at fullspeed. And what I had gotten out of it had been disaster . . . a broken life . . . prison. Everything had been dark and in the midst of that darkness a light had come, a light in the darkness that showed me the way to Christ . . . to God. I remembered Max Jones' prayer.

"Show Frank who You are . . . show him who You are, Jesus." He did just that. He showed me who He was. A scripture I read the day I first accepted Christ came to my mind about someone asking a blind man who healed him. He said, "I don't know. All I know is, I once was blind and now I see." I could say the same thing. I once was blind but now I see. Bunny couldn't say that. Mike couldn't and neither could Louie. I couldn't show people who Jesus was, only He could do that. All I could do was tell them what He did for me and pray that He would show them who He was.

I took down my Bible and opened it and it fell open to the 26th chapter of the Book of Acts, so I began to read.

Paul has been hauled up before King Agrippa and he is telling the King what kind of a guy he had been, how he had done so much against the followers of Jesus and how he was going from city to city persecuting them. At verse 12, he said:

"Whereupon as I went to Damascus with authority and commission from the chief priests, at midday, O King, I saw in the way a light from heaven, above the brightness of the sun, shining round about me and them which journeyed with me.

"And when we were all fallen to the earth, I heard a voice speaking unto me, and saying in the Hebrew tongue, Saul, Saul, (which was Paul's name then) why persecutest thou me? It is hard for thee to kick against the pricks.

"And I said, who art thou, Lord? and He said, I am Jesus whom thou persecutest.

"But rise and stand upon thy feet: for I have appeared unto thee for this purpose to make thee a minister and a witness both of these things which thou hast seen, and of those things in which I will appear unto thee . . ."

. . . and somehow I knew that God was speaking to me. Speaking to me just as if this passage was a letter addressed to me, to Frank Costantino. I was surrounded by his presence and the words echoed in my head as I read them.

". . . delivering thee from the people, and from the Gentiles, unto whom now I send thee, to open their eyes, and to turn them from darkness to light and from the power of Satan unto God, that they may receive forgiveness of sins and inheritance among them which are sanctified by faith that is me . . ."

God was calling me to witness and he was going to give me the power I needed to do it! Hallalujah! This was God's word to me and knowing that it was, claimed it as His truth for me. People were going to hear through me and believe because God had ordained it and He would use me here.

Though the words of the "behavior modification" people had relieved my guilt for a night or maybe a day or two, the guilt always came back and, worse still, I never changed any. Now, with God's promise, the guilt was completely gone and God was changing me . . . changing me more and more everyday.

As each day went by, now, I could see the change. I really never noticed it when it happened. I would just suddenly discover that my feelings about some particular thing had changed completely.

One week I really enjoyed doing something and it was important to me, important in my scheme of things. Then the next week I would discover that I hadn't been doing that any more, that I didn't really enjoy it anyway and it wasn't necessarily bad things either, not all of them. He was just making way and time for other more important things in my life.

Jesus Christ, through His Holy Spirit, was still renewing me! No freight train howled through my nights now. I went to sleep with praise for God and awoke, dreamless, in thanksgiving. A kind of silent, bubbling joy welled up within me and filled my days.

As the days went by I began to see new things around me, things I know had been there all along though I had never noticed them before. The hundred different colors of green in growing things. The shapes of clouds in the sky. The many different sounds of raindrops falling.

I began to see that others around me were in their own prisons, trapped in pain and sorrow, and I was moved. I could feel for them. It was a new experience.

I began to really notice people and what they were

doing. I discovered that inmates in the prison were doing all sorts of things I had never noticed before. Work in the crafts shop, taking extension courses, finishing their high school work, building models of things.

One group of guys, mostly guys who were up for doing drugs or dealing, were actually being allowed to go outside the prison to go to high schools around the area and tell the kids where doing drugs had led them. They were just telling them flat out that if they kept doing drugs, they'd come to prison like those guys did and prison was a bad place to be. It was a fear tactic but it seemed to have some real impact.

We could do that, I thought, and tell them about Jesus Christ, about love instead of fear. Then a singing group came to Belle Glade. I guess Max Jones brought them in. They sang some and then just shared with us how Jesus Christ had come into their lives and what had happened to them.

More and more, I began to think about some of us doing that. We had some guys who were coming to the chapel who could really sing and we had some guys who could play musical instruments too. The idea began to build. We could sing some and then share our own real-life stories. The Lord revealed to me a vision of what we were going to be and, in time, that vision was fulfilled.

Some of us got together at the chapel and I told everybody about what I thought the Lord was showing me and everybody got real excited about it. So we began to work up a format. It was really very simple, just singing and sharing, and we got a guy who played the sax and guy with a guitar.

When we had it down to where we thought we were doing five songs pretty good we asked Max

Jones to listen to the program. Louie sang a solo, a song I wrote for him. Actually all I did was change the words of a popular tune to fit him. The group shared. Some of it looked good and some of it was rough, but Max could see past the rough spots and approved of the program.

He said he would talk to the assistant superintendent the next day about permission to go outside on trips.

The assistant superintendent was a guy by the name of Milo Siegler and he was a tough nut.

I said to Max, "The assistant superintendent? Isn't there anyone else you could talk to?"

Max shook his head and smiled . . . "Frank, if God's in it, who can be against it."

For a minute I lost sight of who was directing who, and it was a problem I was to have many times.

Well, I thought one thing's for certain. If Milo Siegler puts his stamp of approval on this it must be from God.

The following day there was a one p.m. lay-in and chapel call-out for the group. The assistant superintendent had agreed to listen to us and he was going to do it that day.

We set up and every one of the men was doing his best. The program lasted about 50 minutes with the songs and testimonies and when it was over, Mr. Siegler motioned to me to come into Max Jones' office. When I got inside, he said he approved of the group and then he said something that really blew me away.

He said, "I want you to know, Frank, it's you I have the confidence in."

A few weeks later we were on our way to our first outside church. It was a Baptist Church in West

Palm Beach. I didn't think much about it until we pulled up to the building, it looked like a Cathedral. I looked over to Max and said, "How many people does this place seat?" He said he didn't know but it was a lot. I sized up the choir loft behind the pulpit and estimated at least 200 seats there alone.

Some of the excitement of the trip wore off as I thought of getting up in front of a couple thousand people, and a feeling of fear came over me as I learned that the minister, Dr. Jess Moody, was a famous minister. I pulled Max to the side and told him some of my thoughts. "Just trust God, Frank, trust God." Trust God! That's sometimes easier said than done, preacher. I thought the words but didn't say them. Trust God. Okay . . . I'm trusting as much as I am capable of trusting and I still don't feel any better.

Just then the Associate Pastor came up to Max and told him the guest speaker who was to talk about prisons hadn't showed up yet, and that he, Max, might have to give the message. Max was upset. "But . . ." he said, "I haven't prepared . . . I don't have time . . ." "Well do the best you can," he said and left. I turned to Max and said, "Well preacher, all you got to do is trust God" . . . and we both broke out in a laugh. The service went well, it was the first of many times we were to minister for Jess Moody.

One of the places we went was Dunklin Memorial Camp, an Alcoholic Rehabilitation Center run by Micky Evans. He came into the prison right after I accepted Christ and taped my testimony for his radio program. The warmth of the people and the fellowship was great and real. It was a good thing to be with God's people. To be with people who are like-minded. As I shared with them what happened to me they would nod in agreement, and understand what I was sharing.

It wasn't that way with those who weren't God's people. Some of the prisoners I shared with didn't understand or believe. They just had the attitude I was getting over on the Chaplain just to get out on trips and eat free world food. Of course that part was good and so was the going out but it had nothing to do with me telling them who Jesus was.

We were giving our testimony in the John C. Leonard High School one time and a whole bunch of kids were so affected by it they repented, threw away all their drugs and came forward and accepted Jesus Christ as their Saviour.

Some of the other inmates did come to the Lord and I began to see that I had a way of getting to them that preachers from the free world didn't have. I knew what it was like to be in prison. I knew what was happening to them and how it was happening and I could see past all of the front they put up.

Deep down, though, I still hurt over the fact that Bunny didn't believe in my committment to the Lord. Somehow, without me quite knowing how it happened, since I put Jesus Christ first in my life, Bunny had become more and more important to me . . . more important than she had ever been before.

I hadn't always treated her well or honored her in my life but now it was increasingly important to me that our relationship be full and rich and that she know the Lord the way I did.

Time went by and we got a kind of fame about our trips to the outside both in and out of prison. The school kids began to call us The God Squad and the press began to pick up on it and did some features on us.

Soon, I began to have real trouble with some of the guys in the group. There was a lot of in-fighting among them and jealousy began to cause a real rupture. I was going back and forth between them, trying to keep the group together by the power of my own personality, but I finally had to toss in the towel and call it quits.

It tore me up. I wrestled and wrestled with the fact that I hadn't been able to hold it together and I found myself coming awake at night with my mind full of defenses and excuses for its failure. Finally one Friday I just got up and went over to the chapel and went up to the rail and knelt down all alone.

It was a Friday and there wasn't anybody else there. Max Jones took Friday and Saturday off so there wasn't usually anybody at all in there. So I knelt on the kneeler and began to talk with God.

I was angry with God and angry with myself.

"Father," I said, "I tried as hard as I could to do what you told me to do. I just couldn't do it and I don't think anybody else could have either. There was too much going on. Those guys were at each other all the time and You didn't help me any, either.

"It can't be done this way, the way you want a man to walk. If you'd have let me go out and shape those guys up, maybe we could do it, maybe I could've kept them together. It's hard this way, Father.

"Sure, you did it but you're God . . ."

. . . and on and on I went. I felt defeated. As I told God how I had failed, the failure gained weight on my shoulders and I was bowed down under it. In my open confession and my acknowledgement of my guilt, the Holy Spirit began to quicken my mind and to show me the truth.

I had given my life to Jesus but that was all. I had said, "Yes, Lord, I give you my life," but I had never said, "and I also turn my will over to you, Lord." My attitude was, "I'll go for you, Lord, I'll gather for you, Lord, I'll be faithful to you Lord."

I was, I realized, just like Peter in the garden. The Spirit showed me that all of the time I had been running around singing, "Where He leads me I will follow," I had been trying to lead God! The thought really hit home.

I was in front of Christ! No wonder I was getting so much flack. Jesus is the leader. We are supposed to be the followers of Christ.

My prayer changed right there and then, kneeling at that rail, alone, to "I see, Lord, I see. I will follow. I know I can't live the way You want me to on my own."

As I said the words, I felt the presence of the Holy Spirit coming upon me . . . a feeling of warmth and power. I felt as though God was purifying me with a fire that didn't burn and tears began to flow down my face as I felt and acknowledged the presence of God.

I lifted my hands and began to praise him and in that time of praise, I heard God say, "Come back to the prisons and preach my gospel to prisoners."

. . . and I said I would. Somehow, I knew then that I was going to get out of prison. I didn't know how God was going to do it or when but I knew He had a time scheduled for me to get out and that, when I did, I was supposed to come back and minister to the other guys left behind.

In the days that followed, I came to know that Satan was at the bottom of the break-up of the God

Squad and I began to learn something about battling him. The break-up of the God Squad was only a beginning for Satan, though. He soon led me through the greatest temptation it was possible for him to offer me.

Not long after we quit going out to witness, a friend of mine came in the dorm one day, all excited. "Hey," he said, "did you know your wife is here with some guy?"

I didn't and I said so.

"Well, she is and he must be some kind of V.I.P. because the warden is giving him a red carpet tour of the prison and Bunny's going right along with them."

"Well," I asked, "who is he?"

The guy didn't know and we went out in front of the dorm to watch for them as they moved from building to building but just as soon as we got outside, here comes a clerk from the warden's office.

"Hey, Costantino," he said, "there's some Judge here to see you and you're supposed to go to the Chaplain's office to meet him."

"Okay," I said, "who's the guy?"

"I forget," the clerk said, "Judge somebody-or-other."

So I figured it was some judge who'd heard about the God Squad and was pulling some weight around trying to get us to come and do our thing for some group somewhere. Well, by now he ought to know the God Squad had folded up.

When I got over there, the warden had left and the chaplain told me I had special visitors and then he left Bunny and the judge and me in his office and shut the door.

Bunny was really bubbling with excitement and

we talked about the kids for a few minutes.

The judge, who turned out to be a guy I'd known for a long time, was a former judge, but one with a great deal of political clout. It seems some friends were in town and concerned about how I could be helped out of my trouble.

Some moves had been made through a local political leader who was strong in Florida government. "The pork-choppers," they called them and the long and the short of it was a patch had been made.

"I'm on a tight schedule," he said, "I've got to go to Tallahassee when I leave you. Let me go through this with you."

"That's fine with me," I said. I really wanted to know what was up by now.

"Frank, a couple of friends of yours have been talking to me," he said, and he named the guys. "Do you know who they are?"

"Sure I know who they are," I said. "Why?"

"Well, they are willing to put up the money necessary for you to get a parole. They want you to know the amount, and what it's for."

"Parole!" They could buy a parole! Wow! My head spun with the possibilities which were pouring through my brain. Bunny jumped up out of her chair and came and threw her arms around me and there were tears of joy in her eyes.

Wow! I'm through it! I'm through it! I couldn't think of anything else except that I had built all of this time and now I wasn't going to have to build any more. I was through it! It was like coming around the last curve in a long tunnel and seeing the daylight flooding in at the other end.

The Judge's voice broke through my excitement,

"They have to lay out a lot of money for this, Frank, and they want you to agree it's a debt that you owe."

"I understand," I said.

I knew better than he knew and anger surged up inside me as I began to think of what that might involve. I began to see a picture of me going to pay my debt and the guy I saw wasn't the Frank Costantino who had walked in that chapel door ten minutes ago, it was the Frank Costantino who had come to court that morning in Miami, convinced he would never be convicted and even more convinced that if he were convicted, he'd never serve a day of the time.

The adrenaline was pumping. I felt as if somebody had swung one of those big, curved oriental swords with the blade about six inches wide at my head and had just barely missed.

"Judge," I said, "I thank you. I thank you for your interest in me and in my family," and here I took a deep breath, "but I'm a Christian now. I've given my life to Jesus Christ."

The judge looked startled and he paled.

"What I'm about to say now, Judge, my wife might think this is very cruel to her, but for the first time in my life, I have peace of mind and I'd rather do every day of those twenty-two years with Jesus than to walk out of here without Him and leave Him behind."

I walked over to Bunny, kissed her, walked to the door and turned back into the room, looking at the judge one last time.

"Tell my friends I said thank you, but no thank you."

. . . and I turned around and walked out of that office and back to my dorm.

BOOK 2

As told to Joanne Jacquart

16

Leaving "C" Dorm, I hurried past the cafeteria and the laundry, towards the chapel just outside the visiting area in the southeast corner of the compound. It had been one and a half years since I turned down the judge's offer. After serving four years on my 22½-year sentence for burglary, I was being sent to Kissimmee, Florida, on work release.

I entered the chapel, listening to the sound of my footsteps reverberating off the bare wooden floor and benches. A few scattered pictures drawn by inmates failed in their attempt to brighten the dull prison-gray walls. I took a deep breath and knocked loudly on Max's office door.

"Come in! Come in!"

I opened the door and Max jumped up from behind his desk. "Frank! I heard the good news! You're on your way out! How do you feel?"

I deadpanned him. "Fine," I said, "I feel just fine."

We both sat down and Max handed me a cup of coffee. I looked at Max, his hefty six-foot frame topped with a shock of silver-gray hair, a veteran of World War II awarded medals for bravery, and I thought of the many times we had knelt in prayer together asking God to open the prison doors for me. The day had finally arrived. God had honored my step of commitment to follow Him and to do things right this time around. Many of my friends thought I was crazy when I turned down the judge, but it had paid off and now I had a fresh start with no favors owed.

I glanced around this little cluttered office and memories were triggered in my mind—some good, some hard. I thought of the time Max called me into this office, shortly after the incident with the judge, and handed me a letter from Bunny.

"I'm afraid it's bad news," he said.

I unfolded the letter and began reading, "Dear Frank, I'm writing this letter to you so that you will hear this from me first. I met another man and he..."

A sick, numb feeling gripped my gut. "Things have been hard on her," I heard myself say to Max, trying to sound casual.

Max stared at me for a moment, sighed, and decided not to press the issue. Why is it so hard to let another person see our pain? Hiding it only imprisons our soul. I recalled something Emerson wrote: "He has seen but half the universe, who has not seen the house of sorrow and pain." I told myself to embrace the pain and absorb it into my body. It seemed crazy, but I didn't know how else to handle it.

"Frank, do you remember the time..."

Max's words snapped me out of my memories, back into the present.

"...the time we knelt down in this office and prayed for my grandson Ty to be returned?"

"How could I forget? We both challenged God's Word on that one," I grinned.

Caroline, Max's daughter, and her husband had separated. One night when Caroline was attending her brother's wedding, her husband came and took their son Ty from the babysitter.

Many months went by before Ty was found unharmed and returned to his mother. The strain of these months had shown on Max and the Christian inmates had the opportunity to give a little back, praying for him daily and encouraging him. It had brought us all closer together.

We spent a few more minutes talking about the past; then it was time for me to leave. I got up and hugged this rugged man of God who had become like a father to me.

"I want to give a word of advice to you, Frank. When you get out of prison, seek out men called of God."

"I will, Max," I responded.

As I started out the door, he said to me, "Be real, Frank. Be real."

The white prison transportation van pulled up and six prisoners were herded on board. I settled into one of the seats, knowing it would be a long, hot drive. A direct trip from Belle Glade to Kissimmee Road Prison is about three hours, but we had to stop at several other institutions to drop off inmates, and pick up others.

One prisoner began to talk about his wife and how he would be getting back together with her when he got out. My thoughts drifted to Bunny. She had broken off with the other guy and had gone up to Boston to live with my mother. I wondered if it was possible for us to give it another try. It seemed like a long shot and I got frustrated trying to analyze it all.

Max had said to "be real." But I felt like two different people. The one I projected, and the person I really was. I guess in order to "be real," we need to confess our unrealness. Part of me accepted the fact that Bunny had a difficult time surviving while I was in prison, and another part of me wanted to kill the guy she dated. Were both parts of me real? Was one becoming more real than the other as God worked in my life?

Everyone copes in their own way, but most ways are nothing more than escape. Drug abuse is an escape, booze is an escape, even movies are an escape. My way of coping and gaining acceptance had been through success. A Cadillac was a status symbol of success, so I bought a Cadillac. If I had more than the next guy, then I was doing okay. And if someone did something I didn't like, I'd hurt them.

There had been a lot of hate and vengeance inside of me. Was it still there? How much of it was still there? Did I really want to know?

What's the difference between "being real" and being open? I questioned whether or not I even wanted to be open. I like my privacy. But is privacy just another word for secret? And secret another word for darkness? I don't want anyone shining light into my darkness. At least not some corners of it. "Being real" carries a price tag I'm not sure I'm willing to pay.

Socrates was considered a real heavyweight when he said, "I know that I don't know." How profound! What trash! Who cares what he said; he committed suicide when he was in prison.

I need to understand myself. A failure to know who I am creates a vacuum in me that quickly fills with half-truths. I need to be single-minded in my commitment. "A house divided against itself cannot stand."

"Hey, Costantino, get it together," the guard yelled, snapping me out of my thoughts. "Your stop is next."

I looked out the van window. Cow pastures as far as the eye could see. A pick-up truck, with guns mounted in the back window, passed us. Its bumper sticker caught my eye. "Keep America clean. Dip a hippie."

"Oh no," I groaned. "What am I in for now?"

17

We left the main highway and drove for two more miles down a secondary road. Isolated, at the end of the road was Kissimmee Road Prison, my new home. It housed 60 inmates and was in the process of being converted from a road prison to a Community Correctional Center.

My first morning there I worked on the side of the highway with the road gang. I had no choice. Everyone worked until their paperwork cleared Tallahassee and they were free to get an outside job on work-release. This could take anywhere from a few days to a month.

I immediately found myself fighting negative thoughts. What if the parole board changed its mind? What if a new warrant came in? I kept telling myself to think positive.

Captain A. L. McCall called me into his office one day. A 30-year veteran of the Florida prison system, he was the boss here. He carried his tall, broad-shouldered frame with confidence and authority. His thick, white hair gave him the nickname, "Snow."

"Your papers came in, Costantino. You have two choices. Take this job opening at Graves Construction Company as a laborer, or continue working on the road gang until another approved job comes in."

"How much does it pay?" I asked.

"$2.00 per hour."

I'd have to work all week just to earn less money than I used to pay for a pair of shoes.

"Well, what'll it be? Graves Construction or the road gang?"

"I'll take it," I answered. Who knows how long it might be before another 'approved' job turned up.

The June sunshine was bright and sticky-hot. The crew I was assigned to was putting in concrete slabs. My job was to run the Georgia backhoe (hillbilly slang for a shovel). Here I was, someone who had stolen millions of dollars, laboring for sub-standard wages.

Sweaty, thirsty and hot, I tried to deal with my frustration by working even harder. My back ached and blisters appeared on my hands.

The owner of the company came by to check on our work progress. He was short, wore a crew cut, and had a permanent scowl on his face.

"Good morning, Mr. Graves."

"What's so good about it?" he snapped. He glared at me for a moment and stalked away.

I threw down my shovel. Who does he think he is, talking to me that way? I started after him, but then noticed the other workers watching me.

"Get control of yourself, Frank," I muttered. Forcing myself to turn around, I reached down and picked up my shovel. The soil flew, as I struggled to put on a mask of "everything's cool." It's the same kind of mask I'd seen black inmates put on when talking to white correctional officers. A mask that hides the rage exploding in the mind, while giving an appearance of tranquility. It took a while for my anger to subside and when it did, I felt disgust with myself.

"Be real," Max had said. What is real? The fact is, the guy is a jerk. "Lord, how do I handle a situation like this? Do I let people walk all over me? I hate wimps."

My thoughts drifted to Jesus. Jesus did what he had to do. He came to die and didn't back up. He never ratted on anyone at his trial, even though he was worked over by the authorities. And when he hung on the cross, the first person he promised to take home with him was a guy he met on death row.

"Now that's a man I can follow!" I said with renewed determination to let God do His work in me.

During this time I began writing to Bunny. She was still living with my mother and sister in Boston. As my release date neared, we both felt we needed to give our marriage another try and we made plans for her to move back to Florida.

When "Snow" heard I was trying to put my family back together again, he allowed me to work a second job at a local auction. I watched the furniture that came through and managed to buy all the basics we needed for $100.00. It wasn't the type of furniture we had been accustomed to, but it would do for now.

I rented a house in St. Cloud for Bunny, and she moved in with the kids. With a family to feed, I couldn't afford to lose a day's pay, so I decided to put in a full day's work on my day of release.

"Hey, wake up, Frank. It's 6:00 a.m. Today's your day. You're going home!" The duty officer seemed genuinely happy for me.

I went through my morning shaving routine and gathered my personal possessions. I had waited so long for this day that I thought I would be more excited. There ought to be a brass band, trumpets, a parade or something. But it was just another ordinary day of work.

The responsibilities I now faced sunk in very quickly. I had to work 12 hours a day, seven days a week, just to put beans and bologna on the table. The kids were not used to having a father around and they rebelled against my discipline. We didn't have a phone. I managed to buy a beat-up old car. We were lucky it even ran. The kids needed clothes, so I took another job hanging drywall at night.

One morning I said to Bunny, "I don't care what you buy for supper tonight, but this time let's make it something I can chew...even if shoe leather is all we can afford!"

I often felt beat and didn't want to go on, but then I'd think of Jesus and 'do what I had to do.'

I had to adjust to the different personalities of each of the kids and try to discipline them accordingly. Bunny reminded me that they had just as much adjusting to do as I did and that I should use a little psychology on them and be patient.

One day Bunny and I went shopping with the kids. Lori, our oldest, needed school clothes. Bunny took her and Debbie to one end of the store and I took Tony, Rocco, and Michelle to the snack bar and kept them occupied with a milkshake.

Michelle, who was four, kept spinning around and around on the stool.

"Cut that out," I said. "You're going to fall and knock over the milkshake."

She ignored me and fell off the stool. Her arm knocked the milkshake off the counter, splattering it all over me, the floor, and herself. I grabbed some napkins and began cleaning up the mess.

"Michelle, I'm going to kill you when we get out of here," I said quietly, but intently.

The next thing that could be heard all over the store was a high-pitched scream, "Pl-ee-ze don't kill me!"

When I got everyone outside I said to Bunny, "Forget the psychology." Michelle got her first spanking.

The construction business was booming, and as the work increased, I took on more responsibilities. I worked my way up from a laborer to labor foreman, and finally to assistant to the superintendent. In April of 1972, when Graves Construction completed the project I was working on, I left and went to work for another company.

They had a construction trailer right across the street from where I was working, and I went over and talked with Homer, the project manager. They were building a new hospital in Kissimmee, and the superintendent was leaving in a few weeks. He needed a replacement.

"I'm your man," I said with confidence. "No one can build this hospital better than I can." Big words for a man who couldn't read blueprints.

"I was really looking for someone with a little more experience." He looked at me for a moment. "But I guess I can work with you," he said, shaking my hand.

"Could I take home a set of blueprints tonight to familiarize myself with the project?"

"No problem," he said.

I studied those prints for hours and felt no further ahead than when I started.

The next morning I met Dick, the man I was to replace.

"Hi, Frank. Stick with me and I'll walk you through the ropes for the next few weeks." At least he was friendly.

"Right now we're getting ready to form and pour the concrete slabs, so let's start there."

"Slabs? Did you say slabs?"

He looked at me kind of funny. "That's right."

The walls and roof system were already in place, so I thought the slabs were done. It was contrary to all the standard building practices I knew of. But then, I didn't know much. "Better keep your mouth shut, Frank," I said to myself. "Pouring concrete is the only thing you know anything about."

"Thank you, Lord," I whispered.

"What did you say?"

"Nothing, nothing. I'm just figuring in my head how many yards of mud we'll have to put down and how long it will take."

Work got under way, and I jumped in with both feet. The electricians had to provide three forms of power.

Then came the plumbers. They had to provide a complete oxygen system and vacuum facilities in the walls of each room, in addition to regular plumbing. Trying to figure all this out almost drove everyone crazy.

"Frank," the plumber said, "how in the world am I going to get all that stuff in each wall for two beds when the head walls of each room back up to each other?"

I stared at him for a moment. "Look," I said, "your people bid on this job according to the plans and specs. Get with them and figure it out. I want it done the way the prints show." I walked away muttering about having to work with people who didn't know what they were doing.

It turned out to be a good year. I earned enough

money to get my family settled into a little $18,000 home after I made two small personal bank loans to come up with the $900 down payment. My mortgage payment was $158 per month. My rent had been $220 per month, so this was an improvement, even considering the $50 additional per month required to pay off the down payment loans.

Chaplain Max Jones had kept in touch with us since my release. He had been transferred from Belle Glade and was now serving as chaplain at Florida State Prison. He called one day and asked me to drive up on Sunday and speak at the chapel service.

"But Sunday is my only day off, Max."

"Pray about it, Frank. I need your help."

"I can't do anything to help, Max. I'm still trying to pull my own life together. Besides, I want to forget that place."

"I really think God wants you to go, Frank," Bunny said. "Your going back there will mean a lot to the men, especially the ones who know you."

"Yeah, I know. I just hate prisons."

On my first trip up there, the guard in the tower gave me some lip and it brought back all my hate and resentment. But I continued to go and each time it got a little easier.

When the hospital neared completion, I was offered a job with Southeastern Wall & Ceilings, a large sub-contracting company. The owner picked up me and Bunny in his Lincoln and wined and dined us. In December of 1972, I went on board as general superintendent at $300 per week, with a company car and $50 per week expense account. In charge of all the superintendents, I had to travel to the various projects and be sure everything was running smoothly.

That year I went from general superintendent to

administrative assistant, and finally to vice president and general manager of the company.

One of the women who attended our Bible study group worked as a reporter for a local newspaper. She became fascinated with my story and all that had happened since I got out of prison. She wrote a feature article on me which ended up on the front page of the newspaper.

Bunny's brother, Billy, called us after the story came out and said that he had sent a copy to Pat Robertson, host of the Christian television talk show, The 700 Club.

"Maybe they'll invite you to be on their show," Bunny said.

"I doubt it," I said. "They probably just invite well-known people."

"You're well-known," she kidded.

"Yeah, in prison circles," I laughed.

My work at Southeastern was going good until the owner called me into his office one day and said he wanted to drop the entire paint subcontracting division. I didn't agree with him, pointing out that the company made a good return on our money in that area. But his mind was made up. He ordered the painting equipment to be sold.

I had accumulated some bonus money so I decided to make him an offer. My bonus in exchange for the paint division. He accepted and I opened my own little company, "Frank's Paint & Drywall."

Business was good; I earned $200 to $300 per day. We made a step up in housing, purchasing a 5-bedroom, 4-bath home with 3,000 square feet of living area. I bought Bunny a Buick station wagon and myself a Cadillac. We were finally moving in style again.

18

Bunny ran up to me as I walked in the door from work and handed me a letter from the Department of Corrections.

"What's in it?" I asked.

"I don't know. It's addressed to you. Open it," she said, trying to hide her curiosity.

"Oh, I'll read it later," I said, tossing it on the table.

"But maybe it's important," she insisted, snatching it off the table.

"I'll read it after I take a shower," I said as I headed for the bedroom, turning my back towards her so she couldn't see the grin on my face. Her curiosity was getting the best of her.

"Frank!"

"Okay, okay," I laughed. "Go ahead and open it."

She tore open the envelope and started reading.

"It's from O. J. Keller, Secretary of H.R.S. and Louie Wainwright, Secretary of D.O.C. They want you to come to Tallahassee on a Committee for the Department of Corrections. They want a former inmate." She looked up from the letter. "Why did they choose you?"

"I don't know. Maybe because of the things I've done at Florida State Prison with Max Jones."

The first meeting was held a month later and unfolded a whole new world for me. Politicians and bureaucrats are a breed of their own, especially to an ex-con like myself.

I stepped into the formal conference room and glanced around. Pin-striped blue and gray suits were the uniform of the day.

About 25 people were milling around, having coffee and talking. My old street sense came alive. I watched everyone carefully, trying to figure out who the players were. I wasn't really sure why they wanted me there or what was expected of me. Maybe I would just be a "token" ex-con.

A staff member came up to me and said, "Welcome, Mr. Costantino. I hope you had a good trip up here. Let me introduce you around."

The meeting was called to order. Committee members sat down at the big rectangular conference table as the aides and support people arranged themselves around the perimeter of the room.

Chairman Jesse McCreary, a black attorney from Dade County, explained that the first session was to give the philosophical overview of what he hoped to accomplish, to receive the charge, and be assigned to sub-committees.

"But first," he said, "Let's start here to my right and have everyone introduce themselves."

Each person held some important position connected with the justice system. Then came my turn.

"My name is Frank Costantino. I'm an ex-convict."

After the introductions, the chairman read the ten-point charge to us.

O. J. Keller came up to me after the meeting adjourned.

"Frank, I want you to know that I'm interested in what you have to say. In these meetings we haven't had input from people who have actually experienced incarceration. We want you to be free to tell us how you really feel about these things. It doesn't matter if you're out of sync with what everyone else is thinking."

"Thank you, sir."

"The same is true for me," Louie Wainwright said, shaking my hand.

In the plane on the way home, I read the charge and the other material that the committee members received. How in the world would we be able to accomplish all this? Problems ranged from overcrowding to projected growth and prison staff evaluation. I didn't even know where half the prisons in Florida were located. I decided to call the Department of Corrections and get a map as soon as I got home.

I leaned back in my seat, thankful for the opportunity to be part of something like this, but wondering what difference I could actually make. I drifted off to sleep.

After six months of studying the prison problems, our committee made a report to Governor Askew and we were discharged. However, the experience gave me a solid introduction to the larger picture of the Department of Corrections in Florida.

On a personal level, I started spending more time ministering in the prisons, often taking along friends. We'd get up at 3:00 a.m. on Sunday mornings in order to make the long drive to Florida State Prison in Starke and be on time for chapel services. Sometimes we'd stop along the way and buy dozens of doughnuts for the men in the chapel. One inmate wept because he hadn't had a fresh doughnut in 17 years.

Austin Brown, a former inmate from Belle Glade (now assistant chaplain under Max Jones), called me.

"You know, Frank, with all this talk about reinstating the death penalty, the guys on the row are really nervous."

"I'll bet they are. What do you have in mind?"

"I'm trying to get special permission to hold a Bible study back there. If I can arrange it, would you be willing to come up once a week and lead it?"

"Sounds okay to me." We talked over some of the preliminary details and plans.

A short time later he called back. "Frank, God is opening all the doors for this death row Bible study. Superintendent Leverette said he'd allow six men to be checked out at a time and we can meet in the small room at the end of the tier."

"They won't be shackled and guarded?"

"No, they'll just be locked up in a room with you."

"Austin, I thought every time those guys were moved, they had to be shackled and have two or three guards with them."

"That's the normal procedure. But all of that's been waived."

"That's really heavy, but I think I can handle it. I see God's hand in this."

I threw myself into the Bible studies, feeling that I was in the center of God's will. I felt high on God's power, seeing it operate in this, the darkest place in the prison.

"Lord, you know what these guys need. Give me the right words." Week after week I looked forward to seeing God work on this death row, known as the "End of the Line."

Several of the men had a real experience with God and began getting grounded in the Word. It helped them to deal with the possibility of the upcoming execution.

Mike Salvatore was a death row inmate. His teenage daughter led her mother to the Lord and then shared the experience with Mike. It was obvious to me that God was moving in his life as well as the lives of others in the Bible study.

In the zeal of what was happening, the tug of the ministry became greater than anything else in my life. The ministry, rather than my family, got top priority. I felt in good shape mentally, emotionally and physically. I made good money and I had a good relationship with the Lord. But without realizing it, I had started to slip from God's order for my life and began to lose some of my peace.

I started thinking that maybe I shouldn't be making and enjoying money and that I really ought to be just using my strengths and abilities to help others.

One night Bunny said, "Frank, do you know what my friend Marcia said to me today?"

"What, Bunny?"

"She feels God is telling us to go into a full-time faith ministry. How can she say that when we have so many mouths to feed? We'd have to wait for people to send us money in dribbles and drabbles to live on. I could never live like that...could you?"

"I have felt God telling me the same thing, Bunny. But there are so many unknowns. I haven't put it all together yet."

"Where would our money come from?"

"That's a good question. I guess if God wants me to be His employee, He'll pay me, just like I pay my own employees in my company. I really don't know, baby. But I think it's the direction God is leading us."

"I was afraid you were going to say something like

that," she sighed. "Well, we're in this together, and if that's what God is saying, we have to go for it."

"I'm praying about the timing on it," I said. "I'll have to close down the business. I need to be sure."

"There's something I forgot to tell you," Bunny said.

"What?"

"You got a call today from The 700 Club. They want you to be on their show and share your testimony."

On one of my weekly visits to Florida State Prison, Austin Brown said, "I've got some bad news, Frank. You can't go back to death row." His face was downcast.

"The Bible study has been cancelled by the authorities. They said it's too much of a security risk."

Why did God allow this to happen? Things were going so well. The men were growing spiritually. Several had turned their lives over to the Lord, and it showed in their behavior. Men like Mike and John needed fellowship. It was hell being isolated back there year after year.

Just then Max Jones came in. "Frank, you're just the guy I want to see. I have a man coming out on parole for you to work with. He's at a crossroad in his life and could go either way. Without some kind of outside help, he'll be right back on the streets and into crime. Will you help him?"

"Of course, Max. He can stay at my house for awhile."

All the way home that day I continued to struggle with the whys of the cancellation of the Bible study. I was so sure it was God.

Tim moved into our home and we helped him to find a job. I was traveling a lot on speaking engagements, so we all agreed it would be best for him to get his own place as soon as he had income. An elderly lady close by rented him a room and he continued to stop by and see us.

We were glad to see him get involved in a local church and a Christian singles group. With a deeply bruised self-image, Tim hungered for acceptance. He found it most easily in a woman who also hungered for acceptance. Soon they were sleeping together. Tim drifted from us, but more importantly, from God.

Eventually, he married a wealthy divorcee who put him in charge of her construction company. Tim couldn't handle the easy money that he hadn't worked for. He began running around, drinking, and before long his parole was violated.

Back in prison, when invited to chapel, he scoffed, "That stuff doesn't work for me."

The church and singles group were shattered. They had believed in Tim. "We won't be taken in next time," they said. No more jailbirds for them.

Whose fault was it? I couldn't figure it out and didn't want to think a lot about it, for fear the fault was mine. Perhaps I didn't spend enough time with him. But how could I? I had my business, speaking engagements, meetings, trips to the prisons.

I had been thinking about full-time ministry, but all this put a question in my mind. I needed to talk to someone. I called a priest friend—Al Durrance. I wasn't prepared for his reply.

"Frank, it's been apparent to many of us for some months now that God has a special calling on your life. Somehow, I feel that God is going to do some great things through you."

I just sat there looking at him. "You're serious, aren't you?"

"Of course I am. The next step I feel you need to take is to go to Bishop Folwell."

"I don't know him that well," I said. "I've only met him a few times."

"I'll go with you, if you like," he said.

Bishop Folwell met with us and I shared with him the sequence of events that had brought me to the conclusion that God might be calling me to the ministry. He too, made a suggestion that I wasn't prepared for.

"Frank, I want you to consider enrolling in the Institute for Christian Studies this fall for theological training. Then we can observe you and test your calling."

It was not what I had in mind when I thought about ministry. "I'll pray about it," I said.

Arriving home from the meeting with the bishop, I said to Bunny, "The bishop thinks I ought to attend school and consider becoming ordained."

She just stared at me.

"The bishop will pay the cost of the schooling through scholarships."

"Frank, I can't be a minister's wife. People expect them to be perfect."

"I'm not all that comfortable with it either. We need to pray about it."

That's when one of my old friends showed up at the house.

"Come on, Frank," he said. "Let's just go out together one night, for old time's sake. Man, in one haul, we could make enough money for you to cover your expenses for a year and still have some left over.

You could go to the prisons in style."

"In style? You just don't understand. I can't steal money to support my ministry!"

"Frank, you're right. I don't understand what you're doing. How are you going to live?"

I looked at him for a moment. "I'm not sure," I said. "But this I know. I'm God's man and I'm not going to live the way I used to."

"Man, have you gone crazy?"

"No. I've just seen God do one miracle after another in my life and open up doors for me. Who knows, maybe I can make a difference for some of the guys in the joint."

"Now I now you're nuts," he said as he left.

19

Inmates filled the pews in the chapel to overflowing on one of my Sunday visits to Florida State Prison. Max made a few announcements before the service began.

"...and my final announcement is that I'm planning to organize a choir. I'm working on getting some robes donated." Max turned and grinned at me.

He had already gotten me to donate Bibles, chess sets, a coffee pot, some books, a water cooler, band instruments, etc. When business was good and the money was coming in, giving these things was easy. But now I depend on donations myself. Where would I get the money?

I got up to speak. There was a sense of anticipation in the air.

"How many of you can feel the electricity in the air?"

A lot of hands went up.

"Do you know what it is? It's the Holy Spirit in this place. It's the God of everywhere becoming somewhere. You can feel Him. And He has a message for each one of you this morning."

"A lot of you came to this service for different reasons—to see the women, to hear an ex-con. Maybe you heard things were happening here in the chapel and you were just curious. It doesn't really matter. Whether you realize it or not, you're here by Divine appointment.

"It's time for many of you to quit gaming and get honest with yourself and with God, because it's your soul we're talking about. This is not some juvenile, pretty-boy game for sissies. This is serious business.

"I'm not looking for some temporary emotional response from you that won't carry over to your life tomorrow. I'm talking about a sincere commitment. One thing about being a con, you may not fully understand what being a Christian is, but you do know what's real and what isn't.

"Now I want all of you who are serious about wanting to change your lives to come forward for prayer right now, in front of your friends. No music to tug on your heart strings, just stand-up guys who are willing to be stand-up Christians."

Many men came forward and wept at the altar, confessing their sins and asking forgiveness.

"Trust God, men. He is your source," I said as I stood there, watching many make their first step in faith. The Holy Spirit spoke to my heart, "Trust me for the choir robes, Frank. I can be your source too." I knelt down, feeling very small. Surely God could provide for those choir robes, if I believed.

Jack Murphy waited for me in the back of the chapel.

"Hey, Frank, it's good to see you again. I don't understand why you give up your weekends to come here, but I appreciate it."

"How is all of this affecting you, Murphy? What's going on inside that head of yours?"

"There have been big changes here since Chaplain Jones came, and you and the volunteers you bring with you. At first, I thought there must be a catch to this, but I've been watching you. I've seen you and Bunny get back together. You've become successful in legitimate work. I can see that you're not gaming. It's real."

"And what about you? Is it real to you?"

"You know I've asked Christ into my life, Frank. I just have a lot of things to work through."

"You mean things that you aren't ready to give up?"

"That's part of it."

"What's the other part?"

"Sometimes I wonder if it's God working in your life, or if you've just worked hard since you got out and got some good breaks. On the other hand, the messages you bring are real, the kind I can walk down the hallway with and use. And you've been consistent. That says something to me. I see the brotherhood you have with the guys around you, like Max, Mickey Evans, Ben Harrison, and the others. You're all listening to the same drummer, and I like the band."

Jack left, and the chapel was cleared for count. Max was waiting for me at the door for our lunch date. I wanted to talk to him about something.

There was a lot of discussion at the time about the baptism of the Holy Spirit and the gifts of the Spirit. I had gone to some full gospel groups, only to find out that I couldn't be an officer because I didn't speak in tongues.

"Can we talk about the baptism of the Holy Spirit?" I asked Max. "I have some questions."

"Fire away," he said.

"Max, do you believe you have to have the evidence of speaking in tongues to have the baptism of the Holy Spirit?"

"Some churches believe that," he said. "But in my denomination they hold the position that the second act of grace, sanctification, does not necessarily have to be accompanied by speaking in tongues."

We continued our discussion back and forth for some time. I had met many people who did speak in tongues. I totally believed their testimony. I also believed that I had the baptism of the Holy Spirit because I asked God for it. But I didn't speak in tongues. So I wound up feeling like I was neither fish nor foul.

Getting up to leave, I said, "Regardless of all these questions and doctrinal differences, Max, I think you've got the beginning of a revival on your hands here."

"Thank the Lord, Frank. Thank the Lord."

Driving home from the prison, my thoughts drifted back to Jack Murphy. He was going through a lot of changes, trying to cling to some hope. It's difficult to have hope at Jack's age when your parole date is 2005. The guys call it a Buck Rogers date—somewhere out in space.

Word of the ministry in Florida State Prison traveled to Chaplain Ray Hoekstra in Dallas, Texas. He called me one night at home.

"I want to speak to Frankie Costantino."

"I'm Frank Costantino," I said, careful to point out that my name was Frank, not Frankie. But that didn't stop him.

"Frankie, this is Chaplain Ray. We've heard of the great things going on in Florida and I want to fly out to meet you."

We set a date, and he and his wife, Leola, flew out and taped an interview with me. I shared my conversion to Christ and the events that had happened since that time.

"You have a great testimony, Frankie," Chaplain Ray said. "We're going to feature your story in *Prison Evangelism Magazine.* Thousands of prisoners will read it and perhaps some will follow your example. But that's God's business."

We chatted some more and as I was getting ready to leave their motel room, he said, "You know, Champ, you really ought to consider telling your story in a book some day."

My involvement with the D.O.C. increased. After the executive review committee wrapped up, O. J. Keller, Louie Wainwright, and Chief Justice Atkins called for a criminal justice fact-finding conference in Tampa. About 300 people were there—judges, sheriffs, lawyers, county commissioners, etc. Different issues were discussed, and as a group we focused in on some priorities.

Out of that meeting came a series of criminal justice conferences all around the state. Jim Atkins invited me to speak on occasion. He and O. J. Keller co-chaired the committee, and I became the inmate advocate on panels and forums. These conferences went on for about 18 months, and I had the opportunity to meet and get to know many of the people who were the movers.

From this involvemlent, the governor asked me to serve on a regional council. Working with these local law enforcement and criminal justice people in authority gave me a whole new perspective. I saw the problems locally and how they interacted on a state level. I realized I was working with men that I once considered my enemies.

I also became aware of how little impact church programming had on the decisions of the powers that be. I was frustrated at times, but God gave me many opportunities to share what He had done in my life.

When asked, "What made the difference for you, Frank?" I told them my story.

God had made a difference in the lives of some of the men on death row too, but now that the Bible study had been cancelled, I wondered what could be done to keep them growing. I started thinking about the fact that there were already black and white televisions in each cell. Why not tie in an extra channel through a video player and provide Christian video tapes?

Out of the contacts I had made through several guest appearances on The 700 Club, I managed to get help from CBN. John Gillman, the producer, provided teaching tapes and video cassettes of their talk shows. The money for this came from the CBN Missions Fund. We came up with 'WFSP' for our station identification. Once we received clearance from the prison officials, we were on the air. The response was even greater than expected.

Pat Robertson, after hearing a report on the station, was intrigued. He told John Cardoza, the new producer of The 700 Club, to go to Florida and check it out.

John, along with Jerry Houseman, came to Florida State Prison and talked with Max, Jack Murphy, Bob Erler, and some of the men on death row. Excited over the response of the men, they made the decision to produce a full-length prison special, "Maximum Security."

Pat bombarded me with questions. "How many prisoners watch The 700 Club? How many lives have been changed as a result?"

"I don't know," I said. "Why don't you ask the

men yourself? All I did was to put the video system in like God said to do."

Pat laughed and said, "Well, let's go ask them. Can we get on death row?"

The superintendent gave us permission and we began our walk down the largest death row in America. This gave Pat a firsthand look at this human warehouse of dangerous men. And yet, even in this bizarre world, I knew that crusty criminals were softening to the touch of the Holy Spirit.

We paused momentarily outside the first cell. A black inmate looked up from his bunk, started to roll over, putting his back towards us, then did a double-take.

"Hey, you're Pat Robertson! What are you doing here?" He jumped off the bunk and came over to the bars. "Will you pray for me?"

The word started flying up and down death row. Each cell we passed, the men came up and asked, "Will you pray for me?" We walked further and finally stopped at the adjoining cells of John Kampff and Mike Salvatore.

In the midst of a divorce situation, John had murdered his wife. He was sentenced to the electric chair. John shared with Pat his salvation story and said, "I feel safe now. I know I'm going to be with Jesus when I die."

We moved on to Mike Salvatore's cell. Mike told us he was in for a crime that he didn't commit. His guilty verdict came on the word of one man. Earlier, during our Bible studies, I had shared with him the scripture that says a man should not be condemned on the word of only one witness. I believed his conviction was not in accordance with God's Word. I shared this with Pat while we were standing there.

As we prepared to leave, Pat suggested that we pray. The four of us joined hands. Two men behind bars and two men out on the catwalk.

"Father," Pat began, "I agree that neither one of these men will ever die in the electric chair. Right now we hold claim to Your scripture that says, 'If two of you shall agree on earth as touching anything that they shall ask, it shall be done for them of my Father which is in heaven.' "

I felt strange as I listened to Pat praying and started joining him in my spirit. Why would he pray this way? Was God saying something special to him? As I began to agree with him, I felt the confirming presence of the Holy Spirit settling upon us. Somehow in my heart and mind, I knew that neither Mike nor John would die on death row.

As Pat left the prison, he said, "How can I help you in the work here, Frank?"

"I'd like to place ten more video systems in the Florida prisons," I said.

"You've got it." He shook my hand and about a month later sent us a check for $25,000 to carry out this task.

Some time later, I was having lunch with Chief Justice Atkins at one of the criminal justice meetings. We were discussing the death penalty.

He said, "The only thing I can tell you for sure is that I will never allow a man to die in the electric chair for a real crime of passion."

"If that's your position, Jim," I said, "maybe you ought to check out John Kampff's file. His was a crime of passion."

He looked at me and said, "That's very strange. You're the second man that has given me this name in the last two days."

Surprised, I asked, "Who was the first?"

"Chaplain Max Jones."

I grinned.

Later, John's sentence was overthrown and he was released from death row and moved into general prison population. I don't know the reason for his release, nor do I know that I had any small part in helping. What I did know that day was that John wasn't going to die in the electric chair, and I knew it was God's will.

With renewed faith, I continued to pray for Mike Salvatore.

20

"Frank, I've got something to tell you," Bunny said. "I'm pregnant."

Six kids? "God, give me strength," I whispered.

Our family wasn't the only thing expanding. The ministry was growing as well. However, more invitations to speak and requests for help came in than money. This created a financial crunch.

I remember leaving the house one morning to drive to a prison to minister. Bunny didn't have enough money to cover gas for that day's trip. Should I put gas in the car and trust that God would put food on the table that night? It wasn't an easy decision. I put gas in the car.

When I got home Bunny said, "No money came in today, Frank. We have nothing for supper."

"Set the table, Bunny. Let's believe God to provide."

We blessed the empty dinner plates. "God, you know our needs and you said you would provide. We need food for our family tonight." Doubt crept in, then guilt. I should have used the $10.00 for food, not gas. Missing a meal certainly wouldn't hurt me, but I couldn't let the kids go without food.

I could have made a call to some friends for help, but I chose not to. Was that pride? I really wanted to believe God would provide.

Within about 30 minutes Don Brown, a member of our prayer group, was knocking on our door.

"I just picked up 800 pounds of meat from a cow that I had slaughtered. It's all packaged for my freezer, but Diane and I would like to share half of it with you, if that's okay."

"I'm glad you trusted God," Bunny said.

"Yeah, me too," I said, not telling her of the doubts of a few minutes before.

God also required me to stretch in other areas that were not comfortable to me—like taking Bill into our home. If ever there was a Christian fanatic, it was Bill. When I met him he was a pure zealot for Jesus in Florida State Prison. Incarcerated for child-molesting Bill had come to Christ through our outreach there and the influence of Max Jones.

Bill's face radiated the joy of being born again. He rapidly became a leader in the prison church. Numerous correspondence Bible study certificates were posted on his cell walls.

When the time neared for his release from prison, Bill approached Max about going to a Christian environment on the outside. Because of the nature of his crime, his own family wanted nothing to do with him.

Max asked me to take Bill in. My first reaction was, "No way." A child molestor is at the bottom of the prison pecking order and I wanted nothing to do with him. So often these guys hung around the chapel because no one else would socialize with them. I believed Bill was a Christian now, but I still wanted nothing to do with him personally.

I brought it up at our prayer group and we felt God telling us to help him. Danny agreed to take Bill on as his personal project.

For about a year Bill went to prayer group, always praising God. I never quite trusted him, but just racked it up as my personal problem. Bill's parole officer mentioned seeing inconsistencies in his life. There were pornographic materials and other suspicious articles in his apartment.

I shared this with Danny.

"Frank, could it be that you're overreacting because of your own hangups in dealing with this type of crime?"

"Maybe so," I said. But I continued to feel uneasy.

One day Bill fondled a child in a local department store. The police found his apartment loaded with pornography. Should I have held a tighter rein on him and have gone to his apartment regularly to check it out? Would that have made a difference? Or would he have just run if I did that? I felt terribly inadequate.

About that same time, I discovered Genesis II, a health food restaurant in Orlando. I stopped by to check it out and found that a cult with very confused doctrines owned the place. They couldn't make a go of it because the people in the community wouldn't have anything to do with them.

I noticed there was a hotel across the street and I got an idea. I walked over there and checked into renting rooms at a discount for inmates coming out of prison. Then I went back to Genesis II to see if I could buy them out.

They wanted a $50,000 non-refundable deposit for the lease option. I told them I felt I could make the restaurant work, but I didn't have the $50,000. We met again at a later date and this time they asked for $20,000. I didn't have that either. After six months, they had to close down and I got in for nothing down. I felt that was God opening the door for me.

Now I had a place for the men to come—a Christian supper club. Instead of barrooms and honky-tonk joints around town, Christians in the community could come here to socialize and have fun. We'd serve food and non-alcoholic drinks—smoothies. Local Christian musicians would provide entertainment.

The excitement grew in me as it all began to come together. It would fill a need for both Christians and convicts. I just knew it would be successful.

Life got very busy with this additional responsibility and I felt it was time for me to form a board of directors for the ministry. I needed their help and support. We incorporated as Christian Prison Ministries.

The board felt that one of their first jobs was to keep me earthbound.

They felt the financial risk of owning Genesis II was too great, plus it absorbed a lot of time and effort. But I felt it was a step toward helping convicts adjust back into society, so I resisted their pressure to close it down.

Over the six months that followed, my hours at Genesis II stretched from 12 to 16, and sometimes 18 hours a day. Pressure began to build at home, problems with Bunny and the kids. Physically, I was run down and began overeating. I got so busy doing something for God, I quit spending time with Him. I knew deep in my gut that this restaurant was God's program, but I had no peace.

At one of the board meetings when I wasn't present, the men voted to close it down. "It's for your own good, Frank. This place is killing you. You're never home, you're not going into the prisons as much. We love you, and it's for your own sake that we made this decision."

"God, why?" I asked. "This business of ministry stinks. I don't like the hand I've been dealt."

Suddenly, nothing felt right. I hated going to school. I saw very little benefit from the authority of the church, or being ordained. I tired of people saying they loved me, yet not helping me to do what God wanted me to do. I felt alone, tired and out of gas.

My confusion created a vacuum that fed a growing depression and brokenness.

I turned to God for guidance and He showed me that I had gotten too busy, putting my ministry before my personal relationship with Him. I needed to slow down and get things in the proper order again. The program was right, but my priorities were wrong. As I dealt with all this, things began flowing again and I felt myself growing stronger.

Invited back to appear on The 700 Club, I shared the concept of regeneration vs. rehabilitation. Man's plan only attempts to modify existing behavior, but God's plan—regeneration—is a whole new life. Craig Marlatt, a Christian musician and ex-con himself, came with me. We had met at Genesis II, and now he was coming to the prisons with me to minister in music.

While there, Pat shared how the concept of placing videos in the prisons had really taken hold. They had already placed 80 video players and thousands of teaching tapes around the country.

"I don't feel, however, that God has called us at CBN to be in prison ministry directly," he said. "How would you like to take this over for us?"

"I don't know, Pat. Right now I'm busy going to school. Although my ministry is growing, it's still small. I work out of my house. Where would I store all the tapes that need to be sent out? And what about the money to operate it all?"

"Pray about it, Frank. And let me know what you would need for help."

When I got home I figured out the cost. I'd need a video library to supply the software. I'd need to get other ministries involved who had, or supplied, video tapes that we could use. I'd need an office which meant rent, electric bills, phone bills, and a staff. Although it would be a major step, I felt God meant for it to happen.

About two weeks later Pat was in Orlando for a meeting and I told him I would take over the video ministry, but I would need about $5,000 per month to do it. He made that pledge to help me get started and continued that support for the next five years.

Don, a friend and supporter of the ministry, agreed to put up the money to renovate an office building he had if we supplied the labor.

He rented 1,000 square feet of office space to us at a reduced rate for the first year. We needed four staff people to keep up with everything and that meant I had to begin fund-raising to supplement our entire budget.

The American Corrections Association planned to hold their annual meeting in Denver, Colorado, and O. J. Keller asked me to co-chair one of the main sessions.

I told them what God had done in my life. Also at that meeting, Max Jones received the Chaplain of the Year Award from the Salvation Army. He certainly deserved that recognition.

At the end of each year, I submitted an annual report on the ministry to Bishop Folwell. This had been a fruitful year. In adding up the number of services in churches and prisons, I had spoken and given my testimony over 200 times. While I didn't have detailed records, I could conservatively report that I had led over 1,000 people to salvation.

But it made me wonder: Where are they now? Are they serving God? I could only come up with a dozen ex-cons that were really walking the Christian walk. Where were all the others? Did they have the same experiences upon release as Bill and Tim did? Where was the lasting fruit?

About this time, NBC produced the telelvision documentary, "Scared Straight." Nicki Sarner, working with the local NBC affiliate on community affairs, invited me to a special airing of the film, along with correctional, community, and educational officials.

After the showing, Nicki asked, "What's troubling you about this film, Frank?"

"It's fear-motivated," I said. "Fear doesn't work. I know that for a fact. I lived a whole lifetime with fear. People that fear you don't respect you. All it does is intimidate for the moment."

"Isn't it better to scare a kid to get a point across than to do nothing at all?"

"It's not enough to tell a person what *not* to do. You also have to tell him what *to do.* And there has to be a support system to help him through the change. 'Scared Straight' might warn the kids from good families off of crime's path, but for the delinquent offender, it only digs a deeper pit of condemnation."

Driving home from the viewing, I asked myself how my ministry was any different. Sure, we were preaching a message of love and not fear, but what kind of positive support system were we providing?

Providing an alternative lifestyle by itself is not enough. People need people to encourage them. Particularly in major transitions, like getting out of prison and starting a new life.

Breaking a drug habit that has been there for 20 years doesn't happen overnight. Some inmates can quote scripture, but that doesn't give them a marketable job skill, a place to live, or transportation to and from work.

Expecting a chaplain to train inmates to become responsible citizens while they are still in a hothouse environment is like trying to teach a person to speak Spanish, but not giving him the opportunity to speak. It can't be done.

"God, we still need something like Genesis II. I know my priorities got out of whack, but that doesn't change the need."

I began to get a vision. A Christian training aftercare center where ex-cons could learn job skills, social skills, get an education, and receive discipline and fellowship with experienced Christian counselors. Most of my revelation flows out of my own failing attempts at doing God's will. I call it "Bon Ami Vision"—the window is all clouded up, but then I begin to rub and rub until gradually everything becomes clear.

An aftercare center was exactly what we needed. But then, when I thought of all the hassle it would bring with it, I wanted to forget it. No one seemed to really care about the program anyway. Even the ex-cons. All they did was complain.

I decided instead to concentrate on the work I already had before me. There was more than enough to handle. I had agreed to write my story for Chaplain Ray; I was developing a substance-abuse program with Mickey Evans and Dunklin Memorial Camp; I was helping build a television studio to film teachings on drug abuse for the CBN video network; I worked with Jeff Park at PTL to get videos; Mother Angelica had already joined, along with Peter Lord of Park Avenue Baptist Church; Fred Price from California included his video tapes; I was trying to finish school; I was elected as Chairman of the regional advisory council because Doug Chesire couldn't continue in that position due to his schedule; and on and on it went.

All of this went into my report to the bishop.

"Frank," he said, "we are going to have a Venture in Missions in the diocese. We'd like to give some of the money we raise to your ministry. What would you do with, say, $25,000?"

I was about to answer, but he held up his hand. "Don't tell me now. Go and pray about it and get back to me in a few days."

Pray about it? I knew exactly what I would do with 25 G's. There were eighty requests on my desk for video cassettes, some from the largest prisons in America. With that kind of money, we could begin to fill more of those requests. And yet, I couldn't shake that gnawing feeling, that little voice inside me saying, "This money is for aftercare—a bridge."

Still wrestling with this the next day, I talked with Ted Poitras, the board's treasurer.

"Frank," he said, "it's got to be for the video ministry. This aftercare business is just Genesis II all over again, only with a new wrapper, and you know how the directors feel about that."

I felt somewhat relieved and shrugged off the inner voice. I'd tell the bishop that we would use the money for video cassette players.

Early the next morning, Ted burst into my office.

"Ted, what's wrong? You look like you just got run over by a truck."

"Worse than that," Ted stammered. "I didn't sleep at all last night. I couldn't get your aftercare vision out of my head. Frank, I know this is what God wants that money used for."

I knew he was right. I just wasn't so sure I wanted to open myself up to all this again. That night the Lord showed me in a dream an actual aftercare building under construction. He said that aftercare was not to be my ministry, but would be His focus on prison ministry in the '80's. He also told me to ask the bishop for $100,000.

I went back to the bishop and shared all of this with him.

"Frank, I want you to talk to our Venture in Missions Board yourself. I'll make the arrangements for you to meet with them."

The day of the board meeting I felt pretty confident about my request until I listened to the applicant before me ask for much less than I planned to. He was put through a wringer of interrogation and then turned down. I wished I had some formal report, rather than just saying, "God told me."

When my turn came, I simply shared with them the series of failures I'd had and how that led me to this aftercare vision.

"I don't feel capable of putting this together but I'm convinced it's what God wants," I said. "It may cost as much as $500,000, and I feel that I am to ask you for $100,000. I offer this request to you as a Word from the Lord." Then I sat down.

After a brief silence, one priest stood and said, "If God has truly spoken to Frank, we must do our part.

Either we pledge the whole $100,000, or we don't give anything."

Another stood and said, "I move that we give Frank and Christian Prison Ministries $100,000 to start this aftercare center."

There was no discussion either way. The motion was carried unanimously. Then all thirty members stood and clapped and praised God for this step of faith.

All choked up, I thanked them and hurried out as quickly as possible. God had brought me past a point of no return. Little did we know that day that their decision to help would be the catalyst to change the course of prison ministry in America.

21

On June 23, 1979, St. Luke's Cathedral reverberated with the sound of majestic music as the bishop and priests followed the cross and standard in procession down to the altar.

Bishop Folwell's voice echoed, "Bless the Lord who forgives all our sins."

The people responded, "His mercy endures forever."

"Who presents this man for ordination?"

"We do," said Max Jones and Father Leventis.

The bishop then motioned the audience to rise. "Dear friends in Christ, you know the weight of your responsibility in presenting Frank Costantino for ordination. Therefore, if any of you know any impediment or crime because of which we should not proceed, come forward now and make it known."

"Any impediment or crime." The bishop's words echoed through the cathedral.

Father Al Durrance gave the sermon and the congregation recited the Nicene Creed. Bishop Folwell stood up, laid hands on me, and said the prayer of consecration. Father Leventis ceremoniously placed the red stole vestment across my white robe.

The bishop looked at me and said, "Frank, receive this Bible as the sign of your authority to proclaim God's Word and to assist in the ministration of His Holy Sacraments."

As we went through the motions of preparing the communion, I felt like I was in a dream. It seemed unreal.

"This is the Body of Christ," the bishop said as the clergy received communion at the altar.

After passing the cup, he turned to me. "Take the body of our Lord and feed your people." Then he sat down.

I faced the congregation and right in front of me was Bunny, kneeling at the altar, hands cupped and extended.

Placing the wafer in her hands, I said, "This is the Body of Christ. This is the Bread of Heaven."

At the reception following the service, the bishop said to me, "You know, Frank, a lot of people are becoming interested in prison ministry. Do you have any basic guidelines that I can make available to those interested?"

"Not really," I said. "But I'll work on putting something together."

About six months later I was heading to see Chaplain Ray in Texas with the final draft of *Crime-fighter's Manual*.

"Is that the book, Champ?" Ray asked as I stepped off the plane.

"This is it," I said. "I hope it gives people the help they're looking for."

That night as we completed our review of the manuscript for the book, I said to Ray, "We've worked together on a couple of projects. I've got another idea for you."

"What's that?"

"I think we ought to produce a movie and show

what God is doing in the prisons. People need to see and believe that a man can change. If you'll put up the front money, I'll pull together the details and find a location."

He liked the idea and we filmed "Believe A Man Can Change" at Massachusetts Correctional Institution in Norfolk. The 700 Club aired the movie on their satellite system and our ministry reached an even wider audience.

With continued growth, we decided to build our much-needed office space, as well as housing for the inmates we were taking in for aftercare.

I called my staff of nine together, pointing at the map of Orlando tacked to my office wall.

"I want the location of the aftercare center to be in a rural area near restaurants, with light industry for jobs and accessible transportation." I drew a circle around the area that would best suit our needs.

After checking out the properties within the circled area, we found 3.9 acres with two small houses on it for $60,000. Although it required $30,000 cash up front and the remaining $30,000 in two years, we believed it was the property God had for us.

I went to the diocese, explained the situation, and asked them to advance $30,000 of their pledge to purchase the property. They did, and two years later the state purchased a 3/4 acre parcel from us for $62,500 for a right-of-way towards the building of an expressway, confirming to me that we were where God wanted us to be.

We started taking in men who wrote to us from prison, and at the same time we were trying to find a model program to follow.

"What have you found, Ed?" I asked our staff

psychologist one day.

"Well, there are only two programs that I've discovered, neither of which is working exclusively with ex-cons. One is the Teen Challenge drug and alcohol program, and the other is a community in Belgium."

"In Belgium? That sounds interesting."

"It is," he said. "But I don't know how much of their concept we can use."

"Why?"

"It's for the criminally insane."

"Oh." We both laughed.

Without a model to fit our specific needs, I just slipped into the logic of developing a program based upon how I would like to have been treated when I got out of prison. But we discovered a major flaw. I had never been a drug abuser or alcoholic and didn't have the type of problems connected with that mentality. Most of the men coming into our program, however, did have those problems and we were failing in our attempts to help them.

I looked at Mickey Evans' program for alcoholics. He was having more success in changing people's habits. But they used tough love and heavy confrontation, something I didn't want to do.

"You know, Ed," I said one day at the office, "Max sent me this guy, Bill, a while back. We took him in and failed. But we really didn't confront him heavily with his problems. Maybe if we had used tough love on him, he might have changed."

"Frank, my estimate is that about 85% of the men we deal with have substance-related problems. I really think we need to add a strong substance-abuse program to what we are already doing."

We used resource material from other programs

and tailored it to fit our particular needs. Now when we confronted the men with their problems, the same problems that could send them back to prison, they just said, "Hey, man, I don't need this place," and took off.

I shared my problem with Dave Bachman at an advisory committee meeting.

Dave said, "Have you considered doing what the Salvation Army is doing? Contracting bed space with the DOC? We need bed space badly."

Out of these discussions came a contract-release program where an inmate could serve the last year of his sentence at The Bridge. We were able to house inmates and help the state with overcrowding, get a portion of our expenses covered, and work with the men for a longer period of time.

Feeling good about the aftercare program, I continued to encourage other prison ministries around the country to provide this in their area. I invited some of them to my house for a meeting.

As we sat around my dinner table, I looked at those gathered with me, men that God had changed. Joe Donato, Nick Provolos, Johnny Moffitt, Tony Satriano, Bobby Henderson—all men who in some way had lived off their passion and lust for a place on the top of the heap. If we had met fifteen years earlier, it would have been to plan a big score. Now we met for prayer to get God's guidance.

Although aftercare was the main reason I felt we needed to get together, we found that each of us had a desire to be better stewards of time and money in order to best help prisoners.

Out of this meeting came COPE (Coalition of Prison Evangelists). At our first meeting in Atlanta, 300 ministers showed up from all over America.

One day I received a phone call from Lawson Lamar, who had just been elected sheriff of Orange County. He had helped me as a resource in the writing of the *Crimefighter's Manual.*

"I've got something to discuss with you, Frank. Can we meet for breakfast?"

"Sure," I responded, curious as to what it was about.

He had invited several others to the breakfast meeting as well, so I knew that I wasn't his only agenda. When he got to me, he said, "Frank, now that I'm responsible for the Orange County Jail system, I want to have the best jail chaplaincy in America. How do I go about it?"

"The best jail chaplaincy in America? That's easy. You simply hire the best chaplain in America."

"That's great," he said. "Let's do it."

"Whoa! Wait a minute," I said. "What do you mean?"

"I want you to put it together for me, Frank."

"Are you prepared to help make the contacts in the community and help me raise the money it would take?"

"You put together an ecumenical board of directors, representing all the denominations in the community, and I'll speak to them and help in any way I can."

"By the way," he said, "who's the best chaplain in America?"

"That's easy too," I grinned. "Chaplain Max Jones."

22

I walked into the hotel lobby in Tallahassee and looked for the meeting room for the Governor's Executive Review Committee. In my briefcase was a letter from newly-elected Governor Bob Graham, inviting me to serve on a committee to make recommendations on the long-range issues facing the Florida Department of Corrections.

In one corner of the room, Attorney General Jim Smith was talking to a small group of people. Toby Simon, Allen Ault and Louie Wainwright were in another corner. Allen was the head of a couple of state systems and Toby had won the celebrated 'Costello vs. Wainwright' lawsuit against the state of Florida.

"I'll bet that's an interesting conversation," I said to myself as I went over to pick up my nametag. The list of people invited to serve as members included the former head of Dade Corrections, Jack Sandstrom. He was the one who'd sent me to prison in spite of the Supreme Court order to release me. I walked up to him and introduced myself.

"Frank Costantino. Yes, I definitely remember you. My god, the chief justice called and chewed me out for holding you against his order. Judge Stedman told me to send you to Raiford, or he'd lock me in my own jail! I didn't know what was going on, but I did know that I didn't want you in my jail."

"No hard feelings, Jack. I wouldn't have wanted me there either."

"I've heard good things about you since then, Frank. Keep up the good work."

I liked Jack immediately. Bunny and I became good friends with Jack and his wife, Peg. Only God could pull that off.

One day at the office the receptionist buzzed me on the intercom. "There's someone on the line asking for 'The Godfather.' "

"I'll take it," I laughed, picking up the phone.

"Hey, Frank, this is Jack Murphy."

"What's up, Jack? Got a problem?"

"No, just a request. The chapel guys want to put on a New Year's Eve program like you and Chaplain Ray did at Florida State Prison a few years ago."

"Did you clear it with Chaplain Cornett first?" I asked. I knew Murphy would cut corners on occasion.

"I'm calling from his office. It's great with him."

"Okay, Jack. I'll be up that way next week and we'll talk about the details then. We have a few months to put it together."

Bunny and I felt a sense of excitement as we parked the car in the visitors parking lot at Union Correctional Institution.

"Frank, I'm really glad we're spending New Year's Eve with the men here."

I looked over at her and she was getting misty-eyed.

"New Year's Eve was the hardest time of the year for me when you were locked up." She fought back the tears.

"Come on, now," I said, giving her a hug. "Let's go inside."

Men were packed into the chapel pews, others

stood along the walls, some sat on the platform. Convicts that I had known for years turned out. Some came because they were Christians, some just came out of respect.

The Lord spoke to me in that small, inner voice, "Just receive them. Don't preach or condemn. Let your life speak for itself."

"But Lord, I'm getting credit for a life that You changed."

"I choose to make myself known through people. You are my presence in this place tonight."

The chapel service was a moving experience for all of us. Men were taking stock of who they were, who I was, and the values in their own lives. The Holy Spirit was about His business.

Looking through my phone messages one morning, I noticed one from Huey Perry, formerly the head of chaplains for the Florida DOC, now with the Southern Baptist Home Missions in Atlanta.

"Hi, Huey," I said, returning the call. "What can I do for you?"

"Actually, Frank," he chuckled, "it's Bunny I was looking for. At the Congress of Corrections this year we want to share about the trauma families go through when a son or husband goes to prison. Do you think Bunny would come and share her experience, as well as her work with inmate families?"

"I'm not sure, but let me give you our home number and you can ask for yourself."

As I stepped into the house that night, Bunny said, "I've agreed to go to San Diego and speak."

"You did?" I was a little surprised, but pleased.

"I have to deal with my fears—my fear of flying, fear of speaking in front of an audience. I know the Lord has been leading me in this direction, and I want to be able to help you do what God is calling you to do."

"Oh, and there's something else."

"What?"

"We got a letter today from the governor's office."

"Did you open it?" I asked.

"Of course," she smiled. "It was addressed to both of us."

"You'll never change," I laughed. "That curiosity of yours. Well, what did it say?"

"Now who's curious?"

"Bunny..."

"Okay, okay. We're invited to a cocktail party at the Governor's Mansion." She was obviously excited.

"Let me see that," I said, taking the letter from her hands. "You neglected to tell me the part about it being 'an opportunity to discuss and solicit support for The Florida Bar Pilot Grievance Procedure Project,' " I said, quoting from the letter.

"Well, you can take care of business while I enjoy the Mansion. I'm going to call Peg Sandstrom to see if she's going and what she's wearing," she said, heading for the phone. "Of course, I'll need a new outfit."

"Of course," I muttered.

One day Jim Smith called me with the results of the get-together we had at the Governor's Mansion.

"By the way," he said, "Why didn't you tell me you put in for a pardon? I just saw it on the calendar and I'm one of the voting members, you know."

"Well, because I'm somewhat disillusioned with it all. I really felt God meant for me to apply for a full pardon, but what's been recommended is a partial pardon."

"The only exclusion is not letting you carry a

firearm. The only time they vote otherwise is when carrying a firearm is job-related. Do you need a pistol to preach?" he laughed.

"No, but that's not the point. It's a partial pardon, that's all."

"What is it that you want?"

"To be honest with you, Jim, I feel you guys ought to either give me a full pardon with no hooks, or tell me what it's going to take to get it."

Several weeks later I got a call from a staff person at the cabinet meeting.

"Just thought you'd like to know, Frank. The Attorney General made the recommendation that you be given a full pardon and that you be given specific authority to receive, possess or transport in commerce a firearm."

I fought back the tears as I realized that God had delivered again, just as He promised. And the men He used to bring it about were the very establishment that I had resisted years before. I got out the file that said "Frank's Pardon" on the tab and read through the letters that had been written on my behalf.

"God," I said, "I'm having a hard time with this. I know who You are, and I know who I am and who I was. It's You who deserves the credit, not me."

That inner voice spoke to me, "Frank, it's not accepting the credit that's really bothering you, it's receiving My love. I know you want to give, but you also must learn to receive and really believe that I love you."

I took a deep breath, closed my eyes and leaned back in my chair. I thought of the words to an old hymn: "The love of God is greater far than tongue or pen can ever tell; It goes beyond the highest star, and reaches to the lowest hell."

Thank you, Lord, for reaching me.

23

"Do you remember how you felt the first day you stepped into prison?" I asked a new resident at The Bridge. "What spirit did you feel all around you?"

"Fear."

"And when you stepped into The Bridge what did you feel?"

"Love and concern; people who care."

"You need to know that there's something common to both places, even though the environment is different. And that is that we both have rules. They can be used to intimidate you through fear and break your spirit, or they can be used in love to help you become disciplined and live a fulfilling life. The rules here are for the common good of all."

"But what if I don't agree with some of the rules?" he questioned.

"Then, through the proper channels, try to understand them or change them. But while they are the rules, you need to live within them. The purpose is to set you free. It took me a long time to learn that lesson, and I'm trying to pass it on to you."

He left my office and I prayed that God would break through the rebellion inside him. How well I understood!

The phone rang.

"Frank, what are you doing right now? Are you

busy?" It was Jim Smith.

Surprised, I asked, "What's up, Jim?" Usually, the only time I heard from him was when it had to do with DOC business, and at the moment, I couldn't think of anything pending that we'd need to discuss.

"I'm in town and one of my appointments just cancelled out. I've got a few hours before my return flight. Want to have lunch?"

"Sounds good."

"I'll have someone drop me off at your office. Can you give me a ride to the airport afterwards?"

"Sure."

Over lunch I talked to him about Mike Salvatore and asked if he would take a look at his file.

"I don't think he deserved the death penalty," I said, "based on the evidence in his file." I handed him the folder I had brought with me.

"I'll take it with me and look it over," he promised.

Later that month I appeared on The 700 Club again and Pat asked the audience to pray for a change in Mike's sentencing. Afterwards, letters poured in from all over the country—Christians agreeing in prayer.

Several weeks later I received a call from an aide in Jim Smith's office. They were investigating Mike's case. The prosecuting attorney had doubts; Jim had doubts. But he went to the governor with it. I felt prayers being answered.

One night I was alone in the office catching up on some paperwork when the phone rang. I groaned because of the constant interruptions I always got. I decided to let it ring.

Several rings later, I couldn't stand it and answered.

"Frank?"

"Yes."

"I was hoping I'd catch you." It was Jim Smith. "I've got some good news. Tomorrow morning the governor is going to commute Mike's death sentence."

I tried to speak, but the lump in my throat made it difficult. "Thank you, Jim," I finally managed to choke out.

I hung up the phone. How could anyone not believe in the power of God? I sat there for some time, allowing the tears to flow freely in thanksgiving for a God who cares about convicts.

Driving home that night, in the midst of feeling joy, I also felt pain. I couldn't help thinking of the guys who hadn't made it. Charlie Gibson had stood with me ready to fight when the new kid was threatened with rape.

When he got out of prison, he sent word back to the guys: "The name of the game is 'Rip'. Rip off anybody before they rip you off." He got blown away.

Suddenly I felt very tired. So many needed help. I forced myself to forget about prisoners for awhile and began thinking about the townhouse designs I had been working on with Ernesto, our architect. Working with construction was a good change for me.

Wanting to earn my own salary separate from CPM, I had stopped receiving a paycheck from the ministry. Ted Poitras had put up the investment capital and we formed a partnership for a townhouse development. It made me busier than ever because I still ran the ministry as well, although most of the day-to-day responsibilities were turned over to staff.

I hoped the business would bring financial security for my family. I carried guilt because of the time spent away from them and the kids were fast becoming adults. I cut back on my out-of-state traveling and spent more time at home.

I also wanted to build Bunny her dream house. Ever since our first date, we had talked off and on about living in a beautiful house someday. Now I could provide it legitimately. It felt good.

During a break at an advisory committee meeting one day, I asked Annabelle and Louie, "How can I get you to help me get Jack Murphy out?"

"Give me a good reason," Annabelle said.

"Jack is changing. He's involved with Kairos and other programs. He's kicking over the traces."

"Are you sure?" she asked skeptically.

Louie looked at me and said, "Frank, I get a lot of conflicting reports on Jack."

"I know," I said. "He sees himself as a crusader, but he's knocking all that off. I really want to help him, and I feel he's ready. Will you help?"

"Get me some more information, give me a logical presentation, and I'll listen," Annabelle said.

Later, when Jack was transferred to Zephyrhills, he wrote me a letter: "I've come to the conclusion that if a man is not doing God's business, he's just doing time—whether he's inside or outside."

I talked to Superintendent Ray Henderson and asked how he felt Murphy was doing.

"Frank, I'm so convinced that he's a different man, that if you were to ask me to go to the parole hearing, I'd go." Then he laughed.

I called Annabelle and asked if it would help if Ray came up for the hearing.

"That's never happened before to my knowledge," she said. "The superintendent of a major prison coming on behalf of a prisoner?"

"Well, he said he'd come. Would it help?"

"It sure wouldn't hurt," she chuckled.

The night before the hearing, I went to see Louie.

"Boss, I need your help," I said.

"What do you think I've been giving you right along?" he asked. "What do you want?"

"I need a letter or something from you."

"Letter? A letter is not going to get the job done. All your credibility from these past years is on the line tomorrow with this thing. You're going to need all the help you can get from your friends."

At the hearing, the battle was going back and forth when one of the commissioners looked at Ray and asked, "Why are you here?"

"I want to send a signal to the men in my prison. I want them to know that if they'll get their lives right, I'll go to bat for them."

Then I stood up. "You guys have gotten to know me over the years of coming to Tallahassee. I've gotten to know some of you personally. The reason that I'm here in this kind of relationship with you is because, as of October 21, 1969, Jesus Christ came into my life and changed me. The same thing that happened to me in 1969 has happened to Jack Murphy. If you release him, you'll never regret it."

When I finished, there was an awkward silence. Guy Revell put down his pencil, looked at me for a moment, and said, "I believe you."

The vote followed, four to four. Ken Simmons said, "Well, Frank, I guess it's up to me. I'm going to give you Jack Murphy."

I had to muster all the control I could to maintain my composure. I stood up to leave and Ken stopped me. "Wait a minute, Frank. Come back here."

I went back and stood in front of the parole commissioners. Ken said, "I want you to know that the Florida Parole Commission has been well served by your being here today."

I hurried out before I totally lost it.

Back at Zephyrhills, Ray called Jack into his office and we sat down. It was obvious he had braced himself in case the news was bad.

"Well," he said, looking at me, "do I take the curtains down, or do I leave them up?"

"You've got a parole date of 1986 and you'll be transferred to The Bridge in my custody in the next 30 days."

Jack put his head down on the table and said huskily, "It's over. It's finally over."

I'd had about all the emotion I could handle for one day so I hurried Ray out and we headed for St. Cloud. He was driving me home. We rode in silence for awhile, each in our own thoughts. Then I remembered that this was to be my first night in our new house. We had been moving all week.

We pulled into the long, circular driveway. The bright glow of lights spilled through the windows of the house and I was glad to be home.

"This is quite a place," Ray said, stepping out of the car.

"Come on in and I'll give you the tour," I said.

Ray and I visited awhile, then he left. I was as impressed with him as he seemed to be with the house.

We had an open house that New Year's Eve. It was a special time for Bunny and me to enjoy our dream house with friends. And yet, again, there was pain mixed with the joy. Many friends were happy for us; others were not. There is still a concept in many circles that insists someone in ministry must live very modestly. And this was far from modest. Many comments and stories were flying around.

"It looks like a Mafia Mansion."

"I'll bet he dug up all the money he stole years ago

and now he's spending it."

"Who's he trying to impress? He's still an ex-con."

All the flack was irritating and I began to question my decision to build the house. What topped it off was Marantha, my youngest daughter, coming home from school one day, climbing up on my lap, and asking, "What's the Mafia, Daddy?"

The next morning I said to Bunny, "We need to talk about this house."

"I know," she sighed. "It's all getting to me, too. Sometimes I get angry at the comments."

"Some people have even insinuated that I used ministry money to build the house," I said. "And I don't even take a salary from the ministry!"

"Along with everything else to be done," Bunny said, "I feel like the house has to be perfectly clean all the time with all the people coming through. It's hard for me to keep up with it all." She fought back the tears.

"Do you think moving again will bother the kids?"

"No," she answered. "Debbie and Marantha are unhappy here. They feel isolated. They miss having neighborhood friends."

"We've been here a year now," I said. "It's no longer good for you, me, or the kids. I'm going to put it up for sale. If it's the right move, then it will sell."

Two days later, we had a buyer.

24

I tried to concentrate on the accumulated paperwork on my desk. The constant jangling of the phone didn't help.

"It's Jack Murphy," the receptionist announced over the intercom. "Do you want to talk to him?"

"Put him through," I said, picking up the phone.

"Is everything okay, Frank? I'm hearing a lot of flack about my coming to The Bridge."

"Did you expect anything different? You aren't exactly low profile," I laughed. "Everything is still on go. I've gotten a few threatening phone calls—nothing worth worrying about—the media continually calls. Other than that, everything's fine."

"What about Tallahassee?"

"The governor told the media he was confident in the plan that has been put together for you. He said, 'Sometimes difficult decisions have to be made, but I am confident that this was a responsible decision.' So he's standing firm."

"What about Wainwright?"

"He's standing by his decision. You don't need to worry about him. He's not easily intimidated. Listen, I've got some good news for you."

"What?"

"Sheriff Lamar has agreed to let you work in the jail a few days a week with Max training you for ministry. He told me, 'I'll give Murphy a chance to prove he's real. But if he's a phony, I'll bust him wide open.' "

"That's fair," Jack said. "He won't be sorry."

As soon as I hung up the phone with Jack, Max called from the Orange County Jail, asking me to come speak to the inmates there. I went the following week.

"What do you guys think of the chaplaincy program here?" I asked them.

"It's great! We like it," they said.

"Are the chaplains helping you?"

"Yeah."

"Do you know who is responsible for this program?"

"Yeah, it's you and your ministry."

"Wrong," I said. "it's the sheriff." I told them how it all came together. Then I told them the story of my pardon and the men responsible for it. Next I shared about Jack's parole. "You know, sometimes you get mixed up on who are the good guys and who are the bad guys. You strike out against those in authority over you as if they're the bad guys.

"You act like your old friends on the streets are the good guys—the pimps, the hookers, the players. But what did they ever do for you? Maybe they tried to steal your stuff and flirt with your old lady. Where are they now that you're locked up?

"All I'm saying is, check out how you're living. The time for change is now. Don't waste a big chunk of your life away in a cell like Jack Murphy did. He's back on track, but think of the time he wasted—18 years!"

Leaving the jail, I thanked God for the miracles I'd seen, which reminded me to call Jeff Park at the PTL Club. We were collaborating on a book called

More Than a Miracle, trying to communicate the need for aftercare.

Back at the office, things were going full speed as usual. Mark, our aftercare director, needed to discuss some things that came out of our regular counselor's meeting. Don Brown, our office administrator, had his usual detailed list to review with me. Lori wanted to talk about the upcoming banquet.

Among the dozens of messages piled on my desk was one from Larry Woods, CNN news reporter. He wanted to come down with a crew and do a news profile on me and The Bridge program. He'd heard about me in a discussion with Alan Ault concerning Jack Murphy's possible release. Larry questioned whether men ever really changed.

"If you don't believe that," Alan said, "then you need to talk with Frank Costantino." He shared my story with Larry and now the network wanted to do a nationwide 15-minute news profile.

They spent a week with us, filming classes, interviewing Bridge residents, the sheriff, the attorney general. They left no stone unturned. I was called an "unconventional maverick" but the results of the profile were positive and they titled it "Can Time Change a Man?"

After they packed up their equipment and left, I sat in my office thinking about that question. Time alone doesn't change a man, but no one will ever be able to convince me that God can't change a man.

That night, Bunny and I were having dinner with "Happy Jack" Burbridge and his wife, Carol, Joey Donato, "Nick the Greek", and Jerry Graham. These were all changed men.

After dinner, Joey lifted his cup. "Bless you, Frankie. God is raising you as an apostle for us ex-cons in prison ministry."

"Yeah," Nick agreed, lifting his cup. "To the Godfather."

Everyone broke into laughter.

The next morning Lori came into my office and said, "Dad, can you believe we've sold 1300 tickets to the banquet?" She handled our fund-raising banquets. "This is going to be our biggest one yet!" she said.

When the day of the banquet arrived, I went to the Wyndham Hotel early to make sure everything was okay.

Hundreds of people were already there, milling around the lobby, chatting and visiting with one another. Christian musicians from the local musicians' union had volunteered their time and wandered through the crowd playing soft music.

Max served as master of ceremonies. The sheriff pronounced the invocation, standing there in full uniform. Nils Schweizer, a prominent architect, read a proclamation from Mayor Bill Frederick, proclaiming October 26, 1985 as "Frank Costantino Day" in the city of Orlando. Louie Wainwright presented me with a resolution from the governor and cabinet for my contributions to Florida Corrections.

Then Jack Murphy stood to give his testimony. "One of the most exciting moments of my entire life was 11 months ago—the day I walked out of prison. About 100 men in Zephyrhills came out and prayed with me that morning as I left. I told them, 'This is the day that the Lord has made. This isn't the day that the lawyers have made, or money has made, or programs have made, but the day the Lord has made.'

"As I walked out the front gates, there were the men with their arms around each other in a big circle and a large sign wishing me well, and tears streaming down their faces. The major came to take me out. He cried. The guards in the control room nodded, some with tears. Then I saw Frank standing there waiting for me." Jack had to pause to regain his composure.

"At that moment I remembered something Max had said to me years before: 'Jack, if you'll just do God's business and be God's man wherever you are, in His timing those gates will open. God will open those gates wide enough for a freight train to go through sideways.'

"You can either just serve your prison time, or you can make your prison time serve you. We are a product of our choices. If you want to be a winner, you hang around with winners. I'm hanging around with men like Frank Costantino."

Jack continued on for about 15 minutes. As he concluded, he said, "I'm not the same man that went into prison." He held up his violin and recited Myra Brooks' poem, "The Touch of The Master's Hand":

'Twas battered and scarred, and the auctioneer
Thought it scarcely worth his while
To waste much time on the old violin,
But he held it up with a smile.
"What am I bidden, good folks?" he cried,
"Who'll start the bidding for me?
A dollar, a dollar—now who'll make it two—
Two dollars, and who'll make it three?

"Three dollars once, three dollars twice,
Going for three". . .but no!
From the room far back a gray-haired man
Came forward and picked up the bow;

Then wiping the dust from the old violin,
And tightening up all the strings,
He played a melody, pure and sweet,
As sweet as an angel sings.

The music ceased and the auctioneer
With a voice that was quiet and low,
Said: "What am I bidden for the old violin?"
And he held it up with the bow;
"A thousand dollars—who'll make it two?
Two thousand—and who'll make it three?
Three thousand once, three thousand twice
And going—and gone," said he.

The people cheered, but some of them cried,
"We do not quite understand —
What changed its worth?" The man replied:
"The touch of the Master's hand."
And many a man with life out of tune,
and battered and torn with sin,
Is auctioned cheap to a thoughtless crowd,
Much like the old violin.

A mess of pottage, a glass of wine,
A game and he travels on,
He's going once, and going twice—
He's going—and almost gone!
But the Master comes, and the foolish crowd,
Never can quite understand,
The worth of a soul, and the change that's wrought
By the touch of the Master's hand.

Placing his violin under his chin, Jack began playing "He Touched Me".

The audience stood to their feet and applauded for

several minutes. Chaplain Ray stepped up to the podium. "This indeed is the day that the Lord has made! We've heard tonight an amazing story of how God changes men—miracles in prison cells." Ray was beaming as he asked our friends to continue to support us for the upcoming year.

Then Sheriff Bob Fornes from Osceola County came up to close in prayer, but first he said, "Frank, you received some impressive awards tonight and we're proud of you. But I think the highest compliment that you have been paid came from Jack, when he said that he saw the Lord in you."

On the way out, Jeff Park came up to me and said, "Frank, as much as we hate to miss it, Dee and I won't be able to come to the wedding in December."

"That's okay, Jeff. But Bunny will be disappointed. These wedding plans have been the center of her attention for the last six months."

I thought back to the day earlier in the year when Bunny and I were driving home from work and she started crying.

"What's the matter, Bunny?"

"Nothing."

"What do you mean, 'nothing'?"

"Well, I want God to tell you what's the matter, not me."

"Bunny, don't do that to me. How am I going to know what the problem is?"

"When God tells you, you'll know, and I'll know He told you."

"Fine," I sighed and dropped the whole subject.

The next day was Mother's Day. Lori said to me, "Dad, why don't you and Mom go out for dinner together after church—just the two of you. I'll get pizza or something for me and the kids."

Sitting across from me in a little Chinese restaurant, Bunny began to cry.

"Bunny, what is wrong? Come on, now. You've been down for several days. What's the matter?"

Drying her eyes, she said, "God has been good to us, Frank. Every dream has become a reality—my graduation from nursing school, my dream home, the family, the ministry. But there's one thing that hasn't happened yet."

"What's that?"

"You're going to laugh when I tell you. I've always wanted to be a bride and walk down the aisle." The tears started again.

"Bunny, I don't understand. How much do these feelings have to do with the fact that our son Tony is getting married?"

"Nothing, directly. It's just that anytime I'm around someone getting married, I feel that empty spot in my life. Ever since I was five years old, I dreamed about my wedding day."

"Bunny, listen baby, if this is that important to you, let's do it."

"Really?"

"Yes, really."

"Can I have a wedding gown?"

"Yes."

"Can I ask some friends to be bridesmaids?"

"Sure. Plan it the way you would like it."

"It'll be in December," she said, "on our 23rd anniversary. We'll have to make a guest list. Can I have a reception? And a band?"

We ended up having a full wedding party of seven bridesmaids and ushers, with the ceremony performed by the bishop in the cathedral. A reception for 500 friends followed, with dancing and music. Bunny gave the musicians special instructions to play "Aldila". When we were teenagers we had gone to the movie, "Rome Adventure" and "Aldila" had been "our song" ever since.

Following the reception, we immediately flew to London with our friends Ted and Kay from the ministry and Allan and Donna Dykstra from Massachusetts. From London we went on to Rome.

On our first day there, we hired an Italian guide with a Mercedes limousine. He drove us to the Appian Way where we had pasta and pressed chicken for lunch. I tried to envision what it must have been like for Appius Claudius Caecus to build such a road in 312 B.C. It became the chief highway to Greece and the provinces in Asia.

We asked our guide to recommend some restaurants that were away from the normal tourist attractions. To get to the one he suggested, we had to walk down a long narrow cobbled alleyway with the doorways of shops and houses spilling out onto the sidewalk. The end of the alley opened up into a small piazza, the location of Gino's Restaurant.

Sausages hung from the beamed ceiling, whole fish lay on display, along with olives and olive oil. On each table was a crisp, clean linen tablecloth. The waiters wore white shirts and black dress pants.

Two musicians, one with a mandolin and the other with a 12-string guitar, played in a corner of the room next to a huge aquarium containing large tropical fish. While everyone was settling at the table, I slipped over and asked if they knew the song "Aldila."

"Si," they nodded. I told them we were on our honeymoon and slipped them a handful of lira to play the song.

I went back to the table and joined Bunny and the

others. From across the room came a clear tenor voice singing "our song". For just a moment in time, we were teenagers again, dreaming of our "Rome Adventure".

I looked over at Bunny. Tears splashed down her cheeks.

As we listened to the music, I thought, "What a perfect day! Rome, The Appian Way, Gino's, 'our song'."

I reached over and took Bunny's hand. "It just doesn't get any better than this, kid."

"Eye hath not seen, nor ear heard, neither have entered into the heart of man, the things which God hath prepared for them that love him."

I CORINTHIANS 2:9

ACKNOWLEDGEMENTS

I wish to acknowledge the following for their Christian influence in my life:

Pat Robertson
President, C.B.N.

Chaplain Ray Hoekstra
International Prison Ministry

The Right Reverend William H. Folwell, D.D.
Bishop, Episcopal Church

The Reverend Al Durrance
Pastor, Grace Church, Ocala, Florida

Gordon Strongitharm
Elder, Tabernacle Church, Melbourne, Florida

Reverend Donald (Micky) Evans
Dunlkin Memorial Camp, Okeechobee, Florida

Провалы во времени
(на английском языке)

Подписано в печать с готовых диапозитивов. 8.07.93 г. Формат 84×108[1]/32. Бумага типографская № 1-Б. Печать офсетная. Усл. печ. л. 15,12. Усл. кр. отт. 15,54. Тираж 80 000 экз. Зак. 700.

Корпорация «ПИКОРП». ЛВ № 22. 220141, Минск, ул. Жодинская, 18.

Отпечатано в типографии им. Ф. Скорины. 220141, Минск, ул. Жодинская, 18.